How To
PARENT
your
"Tweenager"

How To PARENT "your TWEENAGER"

DR. MARY MANZ SIMON

A
JANET
THOMA
BOOK

THOMAS NELSON PUBLISHERS
Nashville • Atlanta • London • Vancouver

Published in Nashville, Tennessee, by Thomas Nelson, Inc., Publishers, and distributed in
Canada by Word Communications, Ltd., Richmond, British Columbia.

Examples cited in this book are taken directly from personal interviews conducted by the
author. Names have been changed to protect the identity of the adults and children involved.

The Bible version used in this publication is THE NEW KING JAMES VERSION. Copy-
right © 1979, 1980, 1982, 1990, Thomas Nelson, Inc., Publishers.

Library of Congress Cataloging-in-Publication Data

Simon, Mary Manz, 1948–
    How to parent your "tweenager": understanding the in-between years of your 8- to
12-year-old / Mary Manz Simon.
    p. cm.
    ISBN 0-7852-8197-5
    1. Preteens. 2. Child rearing. 3. Parenting. I. Title.
HQ777.15.S56 1995
649'.124—dc20

94-33799
CIP

Printed in the United States of America.

1 2 3 4 5 6 — 00 99 98 97 96 95

*This book is dedicated
to our three children:
Christy, Angela, and Matthew.*

Contents

Acknowledgments

I would like to express my thanks to these people for their assistance with this book:

Duncan Jaenicke, for encouraging me to develop the concept of "parent in the gap."

Janet Thoma, for broadening my sights and sharpening my skills as a writer.

Kathy Rahn, for professional feedback.

Christy Simon, journalist-in-training, for editorial work and office assistance.

Brian Hampton, for in-house shepherding of the manuscript.

John Barger, Allison Callison, Barb Castello, Pat Dismukes, Dede Farquhar, Darrel Hardt, Laura Jacobi, Mary Johnson, Pam Meinders, Sandy Morris, Jan Noble, Kathy Rahn, Sharon Rodriguez, Al Scharf, Gina Segobiano, Brenda Spitz, Katherine Tillery, Katy Wonnacott, all of whom I interviewed at length, and other parents and educators with whom I spoke.

And, as always, final thanks to Hank for his continued support and encouragement.

Part One

Growth and Development

Chapter 1

No Time to Coast

I needed a break.

I couldn't remember when I had last slept more than four hours straight. My nights were filled with nursing babies, toddlers who didn't want to go to bed, and pre-schoolers afraid of the dark.

On most days, I was official toy picker-upper. Sunday mornings, I crawled under church pews after roll-away cereal. Monday mornings, in the steamy YMCA shower, I shampooed an unhappy preschooler while balancing a toddler and holding an infant. I loved my cuddly little babies, but often, life went downhill after Monday's swim class.

Finally, the time came when my children could read a book, ride a bike, sleep in a bed, and not only use a toilet but flush it. Success! Our family had survived the early years.

No wonder I needed a break. I *deserved* a break.

Just a few years would do, I thought to myself. A few simple years of driving to cheerleading practice and tee-ball games. A few years of high-fives for the soccer goalie and polite applause at piano recitals. Just a few years of peace and quiet. That's all I needed before parenting (oh no!) a teen.

What about you? Where are you on this parenting path?

Now that you're parenting a school-age child, you can enjoy some payoffs of your child's development.

If you are reading this book, you probably have a child nearing the age of nine, ten, eleven, or twelve. Now that you're parenting a school-age child, you can enjoy some payoffs of your child's development. You and your son can laugh together at real jokes. Your daughter can wait, more or less patiently, while you visit with a friend. Your child can recall with you special vacations and birthday parties. You can even take a bath without children staring solemnly at you over the edge of the tub!

You've probably realized that something major has changed: the world of parenting looks different from here. Those shoppers who offered, "Let me help you with that load of groceries because you've got the baby," now don't even give you a second look. Experts staffing the parents hot line at the local hospital know all about toilet-training, but they can't answer questions about name-calling on the school playground. Even the pediatrician has backed off: your child's next appointment is two years away. You might be thinking, *It was sort of nice being able to get my questions answered all the time.*

Let's jump ahead for a moment to when your oldest child turns thirteen. The world of parenting will change again. In some ways, it will seem like *deja vu*. Help and advice will be around every corner. Once again, you can order magazines written just for you. Your insurance company will sponsor a seminar on "designated drivers." Your local police department might mail you a parent's guide to teenage parties. And the worry will come back, too. You'll lie awake, waiting for the click of the front door before the midnight curfew.

"But wait," you protest. "Don't bring up those troublesome teens yet. Let me enjoy these in-between years. Let me coast while parenting is easy."

I understand. You want a vacation before the teen years. You are in between the heavy physical demands of your child's early years and the heavy emotional demands of your child's teen years. One way to describe you is "a parent in the gap." As the parent of a preadolescent, you are living between the two highest-profile stages of parenting. You are in the gap.

But your child has entered a new stage in life. He's too big for the teeter-totter at the park but not interested in just standing around talking with friends. He's too old for library story time but too young for the summer film series. He feels he's outgrown the need for a baby-sitter, but he's afraid to stay home alone for any length of time.

Your child isn't a little kid anymore, but he's not a teenager, either. Your eight to twelve year old is in the gray area between early childhood and the teen years. He is a child in the middle—a "tweenager."

Parenting a Tweenager

During these years, the learning curves for both you and your child will continue to go up together.

As your child practices long division night after night, you learn what kind of support to give him. Since your child likes a snack right after school, you don't nag him to hit the books as soon as he gets off the school bus. You continue to learn about your child, your parenting, and yourself.

What happens if you don't continue to grow along with your child? One mom found out:

"I always asked Kirsten, 'What did you do in pre-school?' During kindergarten and those early years, I made a point to pick her up from school and talk about the day.

"Somewhere around fourth or fifth grade, I stopped asking about school. After all, I was with Kirsten so much. I spent a lot of time shuttling her and her friends to gymnastics practices and meets. In about sixth grade, the coach started to drive the girls in a van when they needed to go somewhere. I was finally free of all those trips in the car!

"Now Kirsten is starting high school. I feel I've lost touch. I'm having trouble talking to her. Where did I go wrong?"

Sue forgot to parent her tweenager.

There's no guarantee that if Sue and Kirsten had talked each day, they could have maintained a high level of honest and open communication. But there's no question that the pattern for listening and talking would have been reinforced during the preadolescent years.

Compare Sue and Kirsten's experience with this example from another family:

"Each summer, before we pull out of the driveway for a vacation, we talk about ways the children can become more independent during the trip. Our family vacation seems to be a good time for this: my husband and I have more time since we're not interrupted by the phone ringing off the hook, and the kids aren't in the same old patterns of yelling at each other.

"When Taylor was five or six, he walked with his sister down the motel hallway to get ice from the machine.

"A couple of summers later, I stood in our doorway and watched him go down the hall by himself.

"When he was about ten, Taylor went to the hotel lobby with his older sister to buy the morning newspaper.

"Last summer, we let him go to the motel lobby alone. If the motel had a game room, Taylor could go there with his sister.

"This year, as a twelve year old, he can do everything by himself: get ice, buy the newspaper, go to the game room, find his way around the hotel.

"Maybe it doesn't sound like much, but every year, Taylor has come back from vacation with more confidence. Looking back now, I can see how he learned to be more independent from ordinary things like buying a newspaper."

You, too, can learn and grow with your child.

Taylor's mom and dad parented their tweenager. You, too, can help your child build on earlier foundations. You, too, can applaud as he masters new skills. And you, too, can grow with your child.

I've done that, even though I was a reluctant learner.

Parenting on the Battlefield

Beginning around seven or eight, our youngest child, Matthew, began to show an interest in military history. He lugged home stacks of library books on the Civil War. Personally, I didn't share his enthusiasm. To me, there's nothing glamorous about war or soldiering. But because I know that children learn through experience, I drove him to the library and trudged after him on battlefields.

I will never be a passionate student of military history, but because of Matthew's interest, I have a better understanding of the events that took place in the United States in the 1860s. But Matthew taught me more than history. I watched him develop good listening skills as we listened to a park ranger on the windswept hills at Manassas. I observed his expanding thinking skills as he asked an insightful question at Gettysburg. And when *I* was tired and crabby on a hot day in Vicksburg, he reminded me to be patient. I grew as I supported Matthew's development during his tweenage years.

Learning to Parent a Tweenager

In this book, you'll identify ways in which your learning curve can go up. In Part 1, you'll learn how your preadolescent is growing physically, cognitively, socially, emotionally, and spiritually; and you'll discover how you can parent effectively in response to her new level of development.

For example, in the next chapter, which covers physical development, we'll address guiding participation in sports, talking about sex, and helping your child deal with the social implications of physical growth. That's the nuts-and-bolts type of approach we'll take through all five areas of development.

In Part 2, we'll take a very practical look at everyday issues. We'll discuss ways to develop a partnership with your child's teacher and describe how you can be a homework helper. We'll identify ways to prevent schedule gridlock and to tame the activities whirlwind. You'll even find encouragement for giving your child the emotional space and permission to grow up.

I must be honest with you: this book will not make you a perfect parent.

This book will give you many insights and practical ideas, but I must be honest with you: this book will not make you a perfect parent. However, after reading this book you will be well equipped to guide and support your child through the preteen years.

This is a book about real parents like you and me with real children like yours and mine.

This is a book about real parents like you and me with real children like yours and mine. Throughout the book, you'll hear from other parents of preteens. These people will speak directly to you, just as they spoke to me in personal interviews. Some of their comments are profound; everything you read will come from the heart of a parent in action.

Each chapter also includes sections called "Mirror Talk." Here you'll have a chance to reflect on your parenting. Your investment in this thinking time will allow you to consider practical ideas you can use as you guide your tweenager.

You have a wonderful opportunity. You can stay in touch with your child. You can support his growth. You can enjoy and learn as your child goes through these sometimes "forgotten" years.

You are a parent of a tweenager. This book will help you see that position as one of passion, power, and potential.

And because you parented through the tweenage years, you will celebrate—not cringe—when your child enters the teen years. You will know where your teen came from because you paid attention on the way. You will know who your teenager has become because you walked with her every step of the way. You will face the future with confidence because your relationship with your child will continue to grow and change even as your child grows and changes.

Join me in the challenging adventure of nurturing a preadolescent child.

Join me in the challenging adventure of nurturing a preadolescent child. This is no time to coast: let's get to work.

Chapter 2

Physical Development: From Child to Almost-Adult

One mom had a memorable introduction to the physical development of a preadolescent:

"The experience began rather innocently: one of my daughters needed a bra, so we went shopping. As we neared the lingerie department, Amy disappeared.

> *"A bare arm emerged from the winter coats and pointed in the direction of the bras and panties."*

"I turned around to look for her, and a voice whispered from behind a coat rack, 'I'll go in the back way. I can't have anybody see me in there.' A bare arm emerged from the winter coats and pointed in the direction of the bras and panties.

"I had no idea what size, type, or color bra Amy wanted, but I started to look at what was available.

"Bzzzzzzz! The dressing room alarm buzzer sounded. Someone had tried to sneak in without being seen by the clerk. Guess who?"

This mom had a rude welcome to the world of preadolescent physical development. Like her, you will probably have some kind of experience that signals big changes are on the way. Let's review some basic information about those changes before discussing the impact they have on your parenting.

Physical Changes

Right now, your child might have some youthful chubbiness in his cheeks; that will change. Over the next few years, the bones in his forehead, chin, and cheeks will become more prominent. His face will appear older. Your child will move from losing baby teeth to visiting the orthodontist. Watch for these signs of growth in your child and his friends.

Motor Skill Development

Your child's ability to coordinate her larger muscles now allows her to ride a bike down the street. She can balance, perhaps somewhat wobbly, on ice skates. Eight year olds generally know how to jump rope, skip, and hop. Children will practice these physical skills over and over in game-playing situations. That's why you'll see second graders busy with hopscotch on school playgrounds or playing "keep away" in your driveway.

Eight and nine year olds have busy bodies. They can climb a rope hung from the backyard tree or somersault (with a slight wobble) across the living room. If your child swims, you'll notice that his strokes are becoming more even, less jerky. Because eight and nine year olds are gaining good control over their large body movements, they need many opportunities to explore what their bodies can do.

Small muscle control is increasing, too: an eight year old can firmly grasp a pencil, can easily operate scissors, and is able to put together small blocks and construction toys. Cursive writing replaces manuscript printing by the time children are nine or ten. (This timing depends almost completely on the curriculum adopted by your school.) An eleven year old can hold a book or pencil in one hand and reach down to pull up a sock with the other hand. Observe your child: you will see how his muscles and various aspects of coordination are all coming together to make his body work more efficiently.

MIRROR
TALK

*What did my child do today that helped him develop strength? flexibility? a greater sense of balance?*_____

_____

*How do I model physical activity for my child? (Do I swim at the local YMCA? walk? lift weights? go to aerobics class?)*_____

_____

*How do I encourage my child to be physically active? (For example, you could say to your child, "It's such a nice day. Why don't you turn off the football game and shoot some hoops?")*_____

_____

*What physical skill is my child learning or refining today?*_____

_____

_____

Growth

Eight-year-old boys appear to be similar in size to eight-year-old girls. However, such major growth is on the way, especially for girls, that you'll notice these changes almost immediately. *Puberty* is the physical transition from child to adult. Puberty includes a growth spurt, maturation of the reproductive system, and associated changes in body shape.

Puberty is the physical transition from child to adult.

The timing of these physical changes for both girls and boys varies greatly from child to child. If you entered puberty at an early age, your child might, too, because heredity influences the timing. But nutrition, stress, body weight, level of physical activity, and other factors can impact the time line as well. What's important to remember is that your child's body will change, and each child will experience puberty in a slightly different way.

Each child will experience puberty in a slightly different way.

Around age ten and a half, a girl begins the growth spurt that will accelerate in the next couple of years. Her hips become slightly rounded. She will lose that straight-as-a-board look.

Because eleven is the average age for the beginning of breast development, some fifth and sixth graders wear a bra. Both girls who develop early and girls who develop late will be very self-conscious.

Anticipate changes in your budget: your daughter may

move rapidly through various sizes of clothing. Shopping for a simple pair of jeans might take several hours. As girls develop hips, for example, they might have trouble finding a good fit in clothes designed for children; clothes that fit comfortably often look more suitable for a teenager. At the other end of the spectrum, a girl who remains flat-chested until her teen years will find the clothing that fits her figure in the children's department; the styles, though, may be too childish for her maturing taste. This can be frustrating for both you and your daughter. Avoid criticizing your daughter's body, regardless of the rate at which she is developing.

Also during these years, body hair begins to grow. Some girls will begin shaving their legs and underarms. Your daughter may also need to start using a deodorant. When the rate of growth slows down, usually around the age of twelve and a half, menstruation typically begins.

Eleven- and twelve-year-old girls might be taller and slightly larger overall than boys of the same age because the growth spurt for boys lags behind that of girls. One of the first signs of growth in boys is that the testes become larger, usually around the age of twelve. The penis grows longer, then wider. If your son goes through this stage during the summer when he wears sleeveless shirts, you'll easily observe one early sign of maturity: the growth in underarm hair. This will first be light colored, soft, and fine. Gradually, the down lengthens and becomes more coarse. Then it darkens. This is just one example of the physical changes your son will experience during puberty. A boy's actual growth spurt, which can be very dramatic, doesn't occur until after these other signs of puberty, usually around age fourteen.

The range of differences in physical development can be seen if you look at any middle school class: some girls might be quite tall and well developed; others might still look like children. Some boys will be a head taller than others the same age. A "normal" group of children will include kids who are short, tall, physically mature, childlike, fast-growing, and slow-growing.

MIRROR TALK

*Where is my child on the physical growth continuum?*_____

_____

*How can I prepare myself emotionally to talk to my child about these physical changes?*_____

_____

*What is my child learning in school about physical development?*_____

_____

*Does the school or our church offer resources that will give me some information that I can share with my child?*_____

_____

How Parenting Changes

The years between eight and twelve are obviously times of major physical development and change. The results of these changes will impact your parenting. Let's take a closer look at three specific areas: organized sports, talking about sex, and social implications of physical growth.

Organized Sports

An eight year old has the ability to kick a ball, the coordination to throw a ball with some direction, and the stamina to run a distance. Because of this, some parents choose to channel their child's physical energy and skills into organized sports. The trend toward children's involvement in organized sports appears to be growing.

Some people are not happy with the current picture of children's involvement in organized sports. Noted child developmentalist Dr. David Elkind addresses this issue by pointing out, "Generally, it is parent need, not a child's authentic wish, that pushes children into team sports at an early age."[1]

A parent who often observed this kind of parental pushing told me, "I see some parents who want their kids to be on varsity tennis. They really push their child with private lessons, clinics, camps, and incredible sacrifices on their part."

"My son was pretty average in sports, and average in sports is not much when you're ten years old."

There are dangers in playing team sports at this stage of childhood. One parent said, "Sports for kids this age are tough, especially the kids who aren't good. My son was pretty average in sports, and average in sports is not much when you're ten years old. Sports was a lot of pressure. He played everything: soccer, basketball, baseball. He liked sports and wanted to play. But by the end of each season, you had never seen such a downtrodden child."

There are alternatives to high-pressure competition. Instructional leagues or classes can help a child practice skills appropriate to his level of development. For example, an eight-year-old tee-ball player who is told, "Keep your eye on the ball, hit the ball, drop the bat, and run," can develop arm strength, quick reflexes, and hand-eye coordination. To be honest, I don't think about exercise and fitness when someone asks me whether Matthew is going to sign up for baseball. Instead, I panic (maybe you do, too), thinking, *Matthew won't make the team. All his friends will be playing. He'll be left out.* But team sports can fit into a wellness-focused lifestyle for eight to twelve year olds if parents and coaches give priority to learning instead of winning.

One mother of girls ages fourteen, eleven, and eight said to me, "I look at an activity to see if it's going to better their ability to get along with people, encourage their body coordination, and further their mental development."

Your child can be involved in making the decision whether or not to participate in a sport. Help her clarify why she wants to be involved. Discuss the benefits. Talk through the commitment that will be necessary, for the whole family.

MIRROR
TALK

*What will/does my child get out of organized sports?*_____

_____

*How will/do I benefit from his involvement in organized sports?*_____

_____

*How can I encourage my child to do her best?*_____

_____

*What can my child learn from winning? From losing? In what ways do I support her in both situations?*_____

_____

Participation in organized sports will probably require a financial investment, lots of time, and good sense. As you and your child think about various options, consider these guidelines:

The primary goal of an instructional program will be

learning that is appropriate for your child's age and ability. A competitive program will focus on winning. Because tweenagers seem to automatically compare their performance with that of others, look instead for sports programs in which learning and playing are emphasized. An instructional program will encourage a child's healthy comparison of her performance today with her performance yesterday, not the performance of peers.

The overall tone, in both practices and games, should be positive and encouraging. This means a coach will emphasize what goes well. Regardless of a team's win-loss record, the coaching staff should build up the team and its individual members.

Safety rules should be clearly stated and followed. Equipment should be in good shape. Your child should learn to use it properly.

All team members should play. A major advantage of organized sports is being part of the team. Your child should have an opportunity to contribute to the group effort.

Talking About Sex

At some point early in the tweenage years, you will need to talk to your child about sex. It could be that your child will bring up the topic. Here are two examples of a child-initiated discussion:

A mom relates, "One day, I casually mentioned to my eight year old, 'I think you look more like me than your dad.' He said, 'Of course kids will look like their moms. They come from their stomachs. How can anybody look like their dad?' I followed up by telling him about sex."

Another mother was on an interstate, driving her two sons to a major league baseball game, when one asked, "Where do babies come from?" This mom remembers,

"The questions were becoming more specific, so I summarized it for them right there in the car. When I was done talking, they both said, 'Oh, yuck.'"

Both parents used a *teachable moment*. Neither parent had intended to share the facts of life at this particular time. Neither parent had written, "Talk about sex," on the family calendar. But both parents were willing to follow up when their children created an opportunity to talk.

If your child does not ask about sex, you will need to begin a conversation.

If your child does not ask about sex, you will need to begin a conversation. Here's the experience of one mother who planned a discussion about sex with her twelve-year-old daughter:

"The school had sent home a little booklet. I read it and planned to have our little talk driving to the mall. We'd be all by ourselves without her little brother around.

"I just started talking generally about sex, and she said, in a very bored tone, 'Mom, I know all that.'

"I just started talking generally about sex, and she said, in a very bored tone, 'Mom, I know all that.'"

"So I asked, 'What is intercourse?' She knew that, too.

"Then I asked, 'Do you know when people have sex?' She said, 'When you're a teenager and you start to date.'

"I almost slammed on the brakes. I was horrified. That's the idea she had from TV. I had to take a deep breath and go over what the church teaches. I wasn't at all prepared for that."

Even though this mom planned to talk about sex, she followed her daughter's lead in the conversation. This is an excellent technique. By asking simple questions, this parent could easily see what her daughter knew and what misinformation she needed to correct. (Of course, it would have been even better for the mother to have initiated this conversation several years earlier, before her daughter had acquired the misinformation.)

Like this mom, I carefully planned the time, place, and script when I first talked about sex with one of our children. I had prepared a long, detailed speech in my head. When I finally spoke to her, my speech had been whittled down to about three questions and five sentences! But I was satisfied that she had the information necessary for this time in her life and that I had begun a positive, ongoing dialogue with her about human sexuality.

Was I a little nervous talking about sex? Sure. I'm guessing that the parents who shared their stories with me were at least a little hesitant to talk with their children, too. It might be comforting for you to know that two out of three parents say they have "great difficulty" talking with their children about sex.[2]

It might be comforting for you to know that two out of three parents say they have "great difficulty" talking with their children about sex.

But discussing sex with your child doesn't begin with him. It starts with you.

MIRROR
TALK

When I think about talking to my child about sexual issues, I feel _____

_____.

The hardest thing about discussing sexual issues for me is _____

_____.

I might feel this way because _____

_____.

I first learned about sex _____

_____.

I want my child _____

_____.

Talking with your child about sexual issues might not be as difficult as you imagine. After all, you've been preparing for it for a long time. Your child might have seen you get dressed or at the pool in a bathing suit, so she's aware of some of the visual aspects of human sexuality. She's spent years observing ways in which you interact with men or women, so she's also somewhat aware of other differences between the sexes. Without being aware of it, you've already given her quite a sex education.

Now, because your child is or will be experiencing all kinds of major physical changes, you'll need to continue what you've already started. Often, eight and nine year olds will be most interested in basic "how" questions. One mother of three had this experience:

"My nine year old came to me and said, 'Mom, somebody told me the only way a woman can have a baby is when a man puts his penis inside a woman. That's a lie, isn't it?'

"I said something like, 'No, that is the only way a woman can get pregnant. The woman has the egg. The man has the sperm. It has to come together.'

"Then my daughter asked, 'Did you and Daddy do that?'

"I said, 'Yes, but we didn't do that until we were in love and married.'

"My daughter asked the questions, but my eleven-year-old son overheard, on purpose, every word of this conversation."

This parent did more than simply share basic facts of life: she gave her child accurate information. She used correct terminology and communicated her own values. She gave her son and daughter the same facts.

When your child moves into the ten to twelve year range, his questions and comments may reflect a more personal base of experience. At the school lunch table, your daughter and her friends might have giggled, groaned, and talked about having a period. Your son might have told a joke with sexual overtones. By this time, physical changes are so obvious, especially with girls, that whether or not you choose to talk about sexuality with your child, he or she will have become aware of many related issues.

One parent of three told me, "I never felt comfortable talking with my mother about sex. I wanted to deal with these things with my children. I knew I wouldn't sidestep the issue."

That kind of up-front approach is admirable, but you might not be quite that comfortable or as goal-oriented. As you think about sex education at home, refer to these basic points:

Increase your comfort level with the topic. Perhaps you'll want to rehearse in front of a mirror or with a spouse or friend. A parent of two boys and a girl took another approach: "I wanted to have open communication about sexuality. I took a parenting class through the PTA. I was much more comfortable talking about it with my child after I had talked about it with adults."

Be honest. You might never be completely at ease discussing the changes of puberty. But your child will appreciate, and probably completely understand, if you say something like, "I'm a little hesitant to talk about this with you, but it's so important that I really want to do it."

You don't need to be an expert. If you're unsure about something, just admit, "I don't know. Let's look it up."

Find your own comfort zone. A mother of a nine-year-old girl said, "I've always told my child the correct names for anatomical parts. Then, she can explain to a doctor or someone else, if she's ever touched improperly, exactly what's wrong or what's hurt." Although this is an excellent approach, you need to be comfortable with what and how you share with your child. What really counts is that your child knows you are available to talk.

Realize that one "big talk" is not enough. As is true with other significant topics, just one chat won't answer all the questions. Learning about sexuality is a continuing process. Your child's puberty simply puts this issue at the top of the discussion list for a while.

Realize that one "big talk" is not enough.

Know what your child is being taught at school. There are many sex education programs. School boards and administrators approach this subject in a wide variety of ways. Find out what your child is learning. You may need to modify information from school to fit your value system.

Be sensitive to your child's feelings. Your child needs to receive basic information in the framework of your values, but don't force your child to talk about sex. I had a brief talk with one of our children and then gave her a book with more information. This was the most comfortable approach with her at the time. One parent showed a family life video from the church library; that felt right for this parent and child.[3]

The way you talk about sex now will lay a foundation for continued discussions as your child moves through the teen years. The way you respect her privacy now will set a pattern for the future. As you've seen, you'll need great sensitivity as you discuss sexuality. But as you'll read in the next section, you'll need a similar type of compassionate approach as you help your child deal with all aspects of physical maturation.

Coping with Physical Growth

Your child's body isn't the only thing that's changing; your child's perception of himself is also changing. This was illustrated so clearly in a conversation I overheard between a twelve-year-old boy and his sister.

"I'm a moy," Brandon said.

"What's that?" asked Erin.

Brandon explained: "A boy growing into a man."

"That's stupid," his sister told him.

This boy used goofy humor to try to deal with the physical growth he was seeing in himself. Your child sees how he's changing physically; others see those changes, too. Your child might become very sensitive about how others view this growth. Here's how one parent learned this fact:

"It was a warm, breezy day. Instead of turning on the clothes dryer, I carried the wet clothes outside. My daughter was horrified when she saw what I had done. She said,

'Mom, you can't hang my bra outside. There's a boy living next door.'

"My daughter said, 'Mom, you can't hang my bra outside. There's a boy living next door.'"

"That boy had been our neighbor for years. And I had often hung out clothes to dry. I had to laugh: anyone who looked at Courtney could see she wore a bra. I don't know how she expected to keep it a secret."

During these years, your child's physical changes might impact her actions or behavior in unusual ways. One mother of a third grader said her daughter would only wear big, heavy sweaters to school, even in warm weather. The girl was afraid that if she wore T-shirts, the way she always had before, classmates would see that her breasts were beginning to develop. A seventh grader would only wear dark-colored shirts so that no one could see her bra through the fabric. A fourth grader would only wear dark-colored jeans or slacks; this girl's period had started during a band contest. She was wearing a white band uniform and was so embarrassed that classmates had seen the stain that she vowed she would never wear a light pair of slacks again. Another girl went to school one morning wearing a bra and came home without it. She threw the bra into the bathroom garbage can after she felt some of the fifth grade boys were making fun of her.

These kinds of experiences can reduce your child to tears or make her angry. She will need your support. A kind word, an extra measure of patience, a quick hug—these can all be signs of encouragement for your child.

During this time of many physical changes, we have the responsibility to teach tweenagers about personal hygiene. Consider this example from a sixth grade teacher:

"I had spoken to a student on several occasions about body odor. I asked him to be sure to take a shower, and he told me that he always does. Well, one day last week another teacher came to my room and asked if there was anything I could do. She had already sent him to the rest room to clean up, but the smell was still unbearable.

"When he came into my classroom, I was floored. He smelled like a man who hadn't showered in days. I explained to him that I was concerned about what the other students might say. I told him I was worried they might make fun of him and that we had to do something.

"I found a bottle of rubbing alcohol (used for sponge baths) and took him to the rest room. I asked that he thoroughly wash his upper body. I guarded the door to make sure other students would not see him. I also gave him some Old Spice deodorant.

"After he was finished, I picked up his shirt. It was the main source of the odor. I took him to the locker room where we keep clothes for needy families and found something to fit him. I again explained how important it was for him to shower and shampoo everyday.

"I think a student in high school would be too embarrassed to neglect personal hygiene. By that age, they know the consequences. At age eleven, a boy just doesn't think there will be any consequences. In this instance, I probably stopped a fight from happening, as this student has been in physical confrontations for various reasons. I'm sure someone calling him 'stinky' would have been enough for him to start punching."

An alert parent could have prevented this situation. Although your child will probably take at least one health class at school, it is not a teacher's responsibility to instruct your child about personal hygiene. Classroom instruction about physical maturation should merely reinforce what you have already taught.

Wrap-Up

Your child's physical development is an area of parenting in which you are both powerless and powerful.

Your child's physical development is an area of parenting in which you are both powerless and powerful.

You cannot change the rate at which your child will go through puberty: you are powerless to stop or accelerate the natural process.

But you can give your daughter information about menstruation. You can tell your son about night emissions so he understands what's happening to him and his friends. You can toss a ball for your daughter to practice hitting so that she'll be more successful at baseball. You can take your son to the park so that he can practice shooting hoops and increase control of his large muscles. In these roles you can be very powerful.

During these years, your child will literally grow before your eyes. Don't wait to discuss physical development until you smell your son's body odor or notice a red stain on your daughter's underpants: prepare your child. A child who understands the physical changes before they occur will cope more effectively with what's happening. As one mother of an eleven-year-old girl told me, "I waited too long. I wasn't prepared; I didn't realize that she knew about sex already. But I'm preparing myself to present the facts of life to my son, and he's only eight. I want him to hear it from me first, before the school."

> *"I didn't realize that she knew about sex already."*

When you and your child understand the concepts of physical maturation during these years, you will have a basis for dealing with many of the other changes that will take place.

Chapter 3

Cognitive Development: Moving Toward Abstract Thinking

Can you visualize the wheels turning inside your child's mind? Your child now is able to think through ideas, reflect on past experiences, and consider various possibilities. What's so amazing is that this type of growth all happens in his head, where you can't see it.

Your child's thinking isn't tied just to his own personal experiences anymore. In his mind, he can move beyond the immediate world of family, which you've shared for the past six or seven years. This is a major change in the way your child's mind works. He has moved forward in his cognitive (intellectual or mental) development.

You've probably already observed that something different has been going on inside your child's mind. You might have noticed how your child can think through situations. For example, my son, Matthew, now shakes his head in disgust when a teammate misses a basket with just fifteen seconds left to play. Since his team is one point behind, he knows that the game is probably lost. At age twelve, Matthew can "see" in his mind beyond the missed shot: he can visualize the end result. Only a couple of years ago, he would have focused on the missed basket. He would not have mentally connected that shot to the lost game.

Here's another example. After supper, your child might run outside to play with neighbors, just as he's done for years. In previous summers, the right-handed pitcher might have slopped and stomped in the puddle on one side of the pitcher's mound, while the left-hander benefitted from a perfect toe-hold. Now, even before starting to play, your child and his friends will work toward a fair solution for both left- and right-handed pitchers.

One mom shared a situation in which her eight and a half year old's new thinking skills helped her get through a very difficult conversation. The child's father had just died. The mom was trying to tell her daughter about funeral and burial arrangements:

> **"Explaining about cremation was tough. I kind of tiptoed around it because she wanted to know about the actual procedure."**

"Explaining about cremation was tough. I kind of tiptoed around it because she wanted to know about the actual procedure. I finally said, 'They just do something special and then your daddy's body turns to ashes.' I couldn't say anymore.

"She saw right through that and asked, 'You mean they burned daddy's body?'"

Even in this painful situation, this child could process the information and then predict the final outcome.

During the years from eight to twelve, your child wants to have a sense of mastery, of being able to learn things and practice new skills. One mother helped an eight year old do this during a vacation:

"On the first day of driving, the older two children had each taken turns sitting in the front seat with a map. I was alone with the three children and needed someone to keep me on the right highways.

"During a break at a roadside rest stop, my youngest, Chelsea, asked, 'How old do I have to be before I can be a navigator?'

"So I took the time, on that picnic table, to give her a lesson in how to read a map. When we climbed back in the car, Chelsea got to sit in the front seat with the map. She just beamed."

You, too, can capture such teachable moments. Your child is now mentally able to combine practical experiences with directions. Use every opportunity to teach your child and reinforce your instruction with hands-on experience.

For example, if your son wants to paddle a canoe on vacation, he can experiment now with kneeling in different ways and holding the paddle at various angles, which influence the movement of the canoe. He can think through the paddling action, visualize the result, then mentally back up and change his grip to get a better stroke. Because his thinking is more flexible, he can make mental adjustments. He can learn how to handle the paddle, get where he's going, and not tip over the canoe.

When you support and encourage your child in this kind of situation, you are helping him feel he can do things well. It's important that your child enters the teen years with this sense of mastery.

Although your child can mentally work through some

things, he probably won't understand all the nuances of complicated abstract concepts such as those related to ethics or politics. His ability to think logically isn't fully mature. His growth in mental abilities is dramatic but not yet complete. You might also see growth in one area of thinking but not in another. That's because your child's mental development, just like other aspects of her growth, will not necessarily be even.

Your child's growth in mental abilities is dramatic but not yet complete.

These new abilities will give you additional challenges as a parent. Now that ideas like justice and fairness are mentally workable concepts, your ten year old will be quick to note that her younger brother gets to stay up later than she did when she was his age. With her new sense of meaning and logic, she can link current events and past experiences.

Now that your child can solve more difficult problems in his head, you might have lengthy arguments about why he needs to carry an umbrella when there's a 50 percent chance of rain. You and your child might negotiate a later bedtime on weekend nights. Your daughter's new areas of competence will also give her a sense of power to tackle sports she's never tried or to challenge parents she has, until now, automatically obeyed. As you think about the various types of daily conversations you have with your child, you'll observe the many ways in which your child's thinking has changed.

MIRROR
TALK

*My child's new mental abilities are reflected in his ability to handle these different/increased household chores:*_____
_____.

*I can tell my child thinks in a more grown-up way because*_____
_____.

*I can tell my child is not completely grown-up in his thinking when*_____
_____.

How Your Child's Mental Development Influences Your Parenting

Your parenting will change in response to your child's new mental abilities. Let's take a closer look at how your child's level of mental processing impacts your parenting in several specific areas: dealing with fears, helping your child learn to memorize, and practicing negotiation.

Dealing with Fears

One dad faced this situation with his eight year old: A new movie had just been released. The film contained no objectionable language, no nudity, and no sex. There was, however, considerable violence. When Ryan asked to see the film, his dad said no. When Ryan asked why, the father answered, "Because you're too young."

This dad explained to me, "The reason was more specifically that Ryan was just at the point of determining what's real and what's not real. I don't want him to have nightmares about those kids on the screen being crushed by a car. Ryan knows it only happened with special effects in

Hollywood, but he still sometimes mixes make-believe with real life."

This father used good judgment. He applied knowledge of his son's mental development in making his decision.

Children's fears change during these years. Your child now has reality-based fears.

Children's fears change during these years. Remember how one night your younger child was afraid that his bathrobe, draped over a bedroom chair, was a monster? Or remember how your preschooler was scared to open the front door on Halloween because the neighbor boy, dressed to kill (so to speak), might hurt her? Young children typically have fantasy-based fears.

Now, your child is afraid of being the last one picked for the volleyball team. She's afraid she won't be invited to a sleep-over with the other sixth graders.

Now, your child is afraid of being the last one picked for the volleyball team at school. She's afraid she won't be invited to a sleep-over with the other sixth graders. A child who hears parents yell at each other, day after day, is afraid her parents might get divorced. These are reality-based fears. In addition, your child can understand the relationship between a cause (a parachute hit a power line) and an effect (a person died).

MIRROR
TALK

I think my child's biggest fear now is _____

_____.

I know my child is afraid when _____

_____.

When I was a child of this age, I was afraid of _____

_____.

The last time we talked about fears was _____

_____.

One parent told me, "The biggest thing last year in fourth grade was that Jeremy's teacher got breast cancer. I was the substitute teacher in his classroom on the day the principal told the kids. We told the class Mrs. Smith would have medicine. We told them she would be in some pain, but we tried to paint an upbeat picture. All the kids brought in a dollar to buy her a present. They felt pretty good about being able to do something, but kids this age know you can die from cancer."

"The biggest thing last year in fourth grade was that Jeremy's teacher got breast cancer."

How does your child's new way of understanding fears affect your parenting?

Talk about fears. We tell children that as they grow up they need to act more grown-up. That's a valid message, but adulthood has traditionally included the unspoken rule, "Don't admit you're afraid." That's unfortunate.

Adulthood has traditionally included the unspoken rule, "Don't admit you're afraid." That's unfortunate.

When your preschooler was afraid of a big dog, she would cry and perhaps hide behind you. When your kindergartner was afraid of school, she might have said, "I don't want to go to school." But your older child might not blurt out, "I'm afraid of playing tag football during recess with the eighth graders. They're so big and rough."

One teacher said, "My fourth graders come in with a little wall that's built up through fear. They feel, 'My friend will think I'm dumb because I ask questions.' You have to gradually wear down the wall that surrounds their fears."

Tell your child about times you were afraid, either now or when you were his age. Start a conversation when you and your child are alone, perhaps when you're driving to a music lesson. You might say, "I used to love playing trumpet, but I would get scared before the music contest. Do you ever feel that way?" Viewing news programs together about world events can offer other opportunities to talk about fears.

Be honest. One teacher told me, "Total reality doesn't seem to affect nine year olds in adverse ways. They push me to be honest, to tell them the truth."

Present life issues in a realistic way. Your child's thinking ability makes him able to understand reality. As one parent explained, "I don't want to burden Todd with society's problems, but he knows kids get bumped off their bikes and their bikes get stolen. He's aware that those situations can happen, but he's not afraid to keep riding. Todd's not so cautious he won't ramp his bike. Safety hasn't hindered him as far as being adventuresome."

"I don't want to burden Todd with society's problems, but he knows kids get bumped off their bikes and their bikes get stolen."

Be alert to fears that might require your action. When dealing with some fears, talk is not enough. Is your child hesitant to stay after school to get help from a certain teacher? Find out why there's a problem. Is your child afraid to go to art class because the teacher embarrassed her in front of the class by saying, "You can't draw"? Talk to the teacher. Is your child afraid of getting AIDS from a classmate? Give your child the facts. (For a detailed look at childhood fears, refer to *Things that Go Bump in the Night*, written by Paul Warren and Frank Minirth and published by Thomas Nelson in 1992.)

When dealing with some fears, talk is not enough.

Another clear indication of your tweenager's increased cognitive ability is the skill of memorization. This impacts many areas of life, as we'll see in the following section.

Helping Your Child Learn to Memorize

An increased ability to memorize is most visible during the school year. Fourth graders walk around the school playground memorizing multiplication tables; eighth graders memorize the Bill of Rights or Lincoln's Gettysburg Address.

Why don't younger students do this? The reason is simple: older children have the mental ability to store organized information and then retrieve it at a later time. Your preschooler might remember the big Christmas tree at Grandma's house last December, or the taste of salt water when you vacationed on a Florida beach. Those are solid, concrete memories. But older children will remember more effectively because they are able to plan to remember—or memorize.

Older children will remember more effectively because they are able to plan to remember—or memorize.

Memorizing is a two-step mental process your child develops and practices during this developmental period. Your child first remembers the information, then he recalls it. You will help your child use both aspects of memorization when you review spelling words for a test. Your child will study the words, first. That's remembering. When you go through the list and ask him how to spell the words, you are helping him with the recall phase of the process.

MIRROR
TALK

One thing I remember memorizing in school was _____
_____.

I memorized this information by _____
_____.

My child recently memorized _____
_____.

He did this by _____
_____.

Memorizing becomes increasingly important to a pre-adolescent. Your child will use this skill repeatedly. In addition, the memorization techniques he learns now can be used and adapted throughout his life. Now is the time to help your child discover the most effective memorization techniques for him. My oldest child is a visual learner; Christy memorizes most easily when she sees facts written down. She will rewrite class notes and study maps, graphs, and diagrams. That's how she memorizes most effectively. Another daughter, Angela, is an auditory learner. If a teacher says something and repeats it, Angela will remember that. Some children memorize through repeated experiences. Others learn best by doing, with hands-on experiences. Encourage your child to discover what works most effectively for him.

You can also help your child develop specific memorization techniques. Here are three samples:

Break the information down into small steps. For example, one mother of an eight year old helped her daughter create a separate action for each line of a poem she was required to memorize.

Draw a mental picture. For example, if your seventh grader must memorize the names of four cities on the Mississippi River, suggest he mentally travel down the River, from Minneapolis to St. Louis, Memphis, and New Orleans.

Categorize. If your ten year old comes home to an empty house after school, he might have three groups of tasks: check in (call Grandma, change shoes, unpack backpack, have a snack), chores (let the dog outside, give the dog fresh water, set the table for supper), homework.

Your child's teacher has probably already shared a variety of strategies to support memorization. For example, one fourth grade teacher has a reputation for "red hot tips." Students learn a jingle for memorizing pronouns, and a song for remembering which side of notebook paper to use first. These are not secrets to getting *A*s on tests but simply techniques for memorizing.

Ask your child what tricks he uses to help him remember. Then ask how his teacher helps students retain information. Help your child identify the various strategies he's learned at school. Suggest that your child keep a list of these techniques in a folder at school or on the refrigerator for use when he's doing homework.

Memorization is a mental skill you'll appreciate seeing your child practice. But the next new ability, negotiation, is something that will challenge you.

Practicing the Art of Negotiation

Negotiating with a child might not seem like anything new. After all, a few years ago you could probably bribe your three year old successfully. ("You can eat a cookie in the car if you're good while I do the shopping.") And you could probably trade or deal effectively with a six year old. ("I can't read that story now, but if you wait until after I mow the lawn I'll read you two stories.") However, true negotiation begins now. You'll experience give-and-take on both sides, and as you work out a deal, you'll see your child's mental flexibility and her ability to think through actions.

Negotiation results in both you and your child coming out as winners.

Negotiation isn't manipulation. Negotiation doesn't mean having a long argument until someone gives in. Negotiation doesn't assume you'll always win. Negotiation results in both you and your child coming out as winners.

Let's look at an example.

You tell your eleven year old that her bedroom must be cleaned by Friday night for her cousins' visit on Saturday afternoon. But your child has already made plans to have a girlfriend sleep over on Friday night. You and your child talk through the options and agree to a compromise: The room will be clean and neat by noon on Saturday.

What was negotiated? The time frame.

What was the end result? Your child had a clean bedroom before your relatives arrived.

This kind of give-and-take is a result of your child's cognitive growth. Keep in mind these seven points as you and your child practice negotiation:

Know your bottom line. Know exactly where you won't compromise. Be realistic as you mentally determine your limit.

Be open-minded. Consider options. Listen to your child: he might come up with a good idea!

Keep it short. Often, the longer you and your child talk, the more you'll go around in circles. Sometimes, the basic issue can get lost. Stick to the point.

Negotiate in private. Avoid turning your parent-child negotiation into a family issue.

Think clearly. Avoid negotiating when you're angry or can't focus full attention on your child and the situation. If necessary, tell your child, "Wait five minutes, and then come back. Let's both think of some options before we talk."

Make your points clear and simple. Remember, although your child has some ability to reason, his thinking is sometimes still inconsistent and he doesn't use mature logic. Stick to the basics.

Restate your joint solution. This step insures that you

agree, closes the discussion on a positive note, and prevents any misunderstandings.

Negotiation is a step toward cooperation. It's worth your investment to model negotiation techniques.

Negotiation is a step toward cooperation. It's worth your investment to model negotiation techniques. In one family in which both parents are lawyers, the three daughters (ages eight, eleven, and fourteen) have been practicing at home what their parents do on the job:

"One of the girls will come to us with a proposal and a willingness to negotiate details. She will plead her case and say, 'This is what I want to do. This is why you might not want me to do it.' She'll say why she wants to do it, and then we talk. I tell her the areas in which I'd be willing to compromise. At our house, negotiation usually happens in situations when a child wants to stay home from a family outing or wants to attend a social function with a friend."

Wrap-Up

Although this new stage of mental development happens on the inside of your child's body, outwardly you'll observe many examples of his growth. He'll use reasoning in a way that's different and more adult than ever before. Usually, you're glad to see this change; but when discussions get bogged down and your child doesn't automatically comply with a request, you might wish you could return to the days of parenting that innocent preschooler.

Your child now can determine the underlying concern for realistic fears. He can use new mental abilities to help him memorize. Negotiation will exercise his newly flexible mind. These signs of mental growth are indications that your child is almost ready to move to the next stage, in which he will develop abstract reasoning.

Chapter 4

Social Development:
The World of Peers

You are probably seeing many signs that your child is developing more extensive social skills. An eight year old knows how to say "thank you" and "please" without being reminded. During basketball practice, your child passes the ball to a team member who has a better chance of making a basket. Without prompting, your child will share a candy stick with her sister. Your child has not only learned that it's good to be around people; she's practicing the social skills that encourage others to interact with her.

During these years, you'll see the very social side of what psychologist David Elkind labels *the culture of childhood.*[1] Your child may join a group of kids who enjoy such varied activities as skateboarding and make-believe play. He'll make up rhymes and chants. Your child and his friends will laugh at updated versions of the same kind of silly jokes that you told when you were his age. Your nine year old will make up goofy nicknames for his sister and discover the wonder of the telephone. The phone will become a major avenue of socialization as your child edges closer to the teen years.

Your child roams the neighborhood with others. When your ten year old comes inside for a glass of water, you know he's in the house because you hear a herd of footsteps. Apples sitting in a bowl on the kitchen table disappear when your child enters the room because he often comes in with friends. So many everyday happenings become social events full of chattering, laughing, and giggling. Your eight to twelve year old is immersed in the world of his peers.

Why does all this socialization happen? Because of your child's development. Your child is growing in the ability to see things from another person's point of view. With your child's more developed understanding of time, your child can begin a friendship today and reasonably expect it to continue next week. Your child can keep a confidence, and "secrets" bring friends together.

Your child is growing in the ability to see things from another person's point of view.

But like all other aspects of development, social progress isn't recorded on a smooth, always-upward learning curve. As one fifth grade teacher told me, "So many parents, every year, request a conference. When we meet, the parents say school is fine and their child's grades are fine. It's P.E. and recess the parents want to talk about. We spend the whole conference just talking about social issues."

MIRROR
TALK

*The social problem that causes my child the most pain is*_____
_____.

I know my child had a difficult time dealing with _____
_____.

My child's best friend is _____
_____.

My child generally chooses friends who _____
_____.

During these years, some children desperately seek popularity. What makes a child popular? One sixth grade teacher put together this composite: "A popular student has good looks, confidence, talks freely in a large group, shows interest in others, is athletic, polite, witty, and funny." Even a child with many of these characteristics might discover the cruel reality that reaching the peak of popularity lies consistently beyond his grasp. In desperation, a child might lash out toward a peer. The most common targets are children they perceive as being "different"—for example, the child who is overweight or the "brain" who consistently wins academic competitions.

But any child can become a social outcast. At a family gathering, your ten year old might become the target of crude jokes by twelve year old cousins. The lack of a particular brand of clothing might deny an eleven year old a ticket into the sixth grade clique. And being in the "right" group today doesn't mean your child will be in that group forever; tomorrow, he might be on the outside looking in.

Being in the "right" group today doesn't mean your child will be in that group forever; tomorrow, he might be on the outside looking in.

Children at this age are very aware they are excluding people from the "in" group. The decision to exclude often begins with a single child; others join the attack because it distracts peer attention from themselves.

Social Differences Between Age Groups and Sexes

Your child's socialization might follow a predictable pattern. Numerous researchers have focused on this topic, but the informal observations shared by one junior high principal provide a real-life glimpse of social life during these years:

"Fifth graders argue among themselves. Invariably, they'll still be arguing after recess or P.E. They can't separate themselves from the game and go to the new role as students.

"Sixth grade boys get along better with each other, but girls don't. There are female-to-female problems. I hear a lot of 'Susie likes everybody else, but she doesn't like me.' Sixth grade girls can be very mean to each other.

"Seventh grade is the most delightful group. They've solved some earlier relationship dilemmas and are at a social plateau.

"Eighth grade is a struggle. The kids are well on their way to becoming adults and are beginning to struggle with the opposite sex and their future plans. Some boys feel they have to be macho, some girls feel they have to be sex symbols; but neither girls nor boys are capable of dealing with either of those roles."

Another school principal might characterize students in these same grades in a totally different way because there are many individual differences. Your child might not fit into any of the neat little descriptions given above. In our family, fourth grade was tough for one daughter, sixth grade was hard for our son, and seventh grade was the difficult year for another daughter. One of the best things about having teenagers is that I won't ever go through seventh grade with a girl again! In one of our daughter's classes, the seventh grade girls spent the whole year complaining and fighting among themselves. As a direct result, a member of Angela's cheerleading squad dissolved in tears at a seventh grade basketball game.

In a different neighborhood, seventh graders might get along well on most days. In yet another school, in-fighting and petty jealousy results in lockers glued shut or stolen gym shorts. These kinds of social-based problems can happen anytime during these years.

Boys and girls become aware of each other in new ways. As one mother of an eleven year old observed, "There's a lot of pressure to pair off already." Twelve-year-old boys might look with interest toward female classmates, who have been watching them for several years already.

Boys stick together. Their activities tend to revolve around sports. This type of activity is far less important to girls; talking about people is what matters. Girls are keenly interested in relationships: a teacher who is engaged to be married or a pregnant coach will be the subject of many giggly conversations.

The balance of social influence shifts as your child spends more time with people at school and after school than he spends at home with you. Peers, siblings, grandparents, the neighbor across the street, members of the brass section of the school band, younger children who ride the school bus, and others are making a mark on your child's social development. You will see many signs of such influence.

The balance of social influence shifts as your child spends more time with people at school and after school than he spends at home with you.

Same-age friends can have a major impact on the tweenager. This is true because your child is responding to peer pressure more than ever before. As one elementary school principal observed, "One fifth grader even got her hair cut like other girls so she could fit into the right group."

"One fifth grader even got her hair cut like other girls so she could fit into the right group."

Your child might experience both the highs and the hurts that come with socialization during these years. Your son might be "on top of the world" when asked to join a secret club. Your daughter might be thrilled to receive a note passed to her during math class. Yet the next day she might cringe to hear cruel words hurled at her: "Only certain girls can drink from this fountain." This type of social exclusion happens more frequently as children begin to choose close friends as opposed to the multitude of acquaintances typical of eight and nine year olds.

Identify Your New Role

The ways in which you support your child's social development will change dramatically. Years ago, you could help the four year old who ran to you crying because, "Jason won't play with me." You could control social situations to guarantee a positive outcome. You could smooth rough edges between six year olds playing tag and help provide a positive transition from one situation to another.

When your child is eight or nine years old, you can still directly influence social experiences when they occur on home turf. Here's an example from the parent of a nine year old:

"A friend from school phoned Bryan and asked him to come over and play. I didn't know the child or his family. Before I said yes, I drove by the child's house. There were a lot of older boys hanging around the apartment building. People were yelling out the windows.

"When I got back home, I told Bryan he could invite the little boy here to play. My son was upset, but I needed to know more about this child and his family before I'd let Bryan go there. The little boy came over here to play while I was around that day, and it went well."

Although you can control to a certain extent what happens in your own home, an increasing number of social experiences will take place away from home. You won't be able to run interference for the eight year old left out of a game of foursquare on the playground. You can't barge into the school cafeteria to force someone to eat lunch with your daughter, who's at a table all by herself. You can't take away the hurt your son felt when he was excluded from the neighborhood game of pickup baseball. When your child is eleven or twelve years old, your support will be more indirect than it was in earlier years. Here's a good example:

"Kim is the kind of person who attaches to one friend. In seventh and eighth grade, Kim chose a friend who was not the kind of person I felt was best for her. It was very hard for me to stand back and say, 'She's made the choice.' But I continued to encourage her to have other friends. When this one person wasn't available, I'd suggest other people. This gave us a chance to talk about how different people can meet different needs.

"Kim understood what we were saying, but she needed to go through a learning process on her own terms and in her own time. I'm happy to say that now as a teenager, she has four friends and is doing much better."

MIRROR
TALK

My current role in my child's social development is _____
_____.

The biggest challenge for me right now is _____
_____.

The biggest social challenge for my child right now is _____
_____.

One way in which I can help my child is _____
_____.

You will see many signs that indicate the need to redefine your role as your child moves through these years. One mom with a twelve-year-old girl and a nine-year-old boy says, "We are just starting to get into name brand clothing issues. I'm beginning to see peer pressure as the kids ask for the right shoes, the right label on the shirt. It's beginning to be important."

"I'm beginning to see peer pressure as the kids ask for the right shoes, the right label on the shirt."

How is this mom continuing to help her children grow?

"We're trying to show that it's okay to have some of those things, but your whole identity shouldn't revolve around wearing the kind of shoes your friend has. We reinforce that's not as important as other things. Clothes are just a tiny part of a person."

This mom has recognized the importance of her children's peer group influence but is trying to keep that influence in a proper perspective. She's trying to strike a balance between her children's desire to fit in and the family value system.

Convey to your child that there will be a tomorrow.

However you define your role, share with your child a vision for the future. As your child works through various social situations, convey to him that there will be a tomorrow. This can be tough, especially when you're dealing with a child who forgot his locker combination and is afraid to go to school tomorrow because he's sure all the kids will laugh at him. Help your child understand these four points:

Socialization is a process. Working through problems with friends and finding your personal niche in a class or group is a normal, natural part of growing up. Things will not necessarily fit together like puzzle pieces.

You will support him and listen to him. When your child tells you what is happening, show your care and support.

Even troublesome situations might be resolved in the future. Help your child acknowledge the possibility of a long-distance perspective.

Every situation won't have a fairy-tale ending. A tweenager gradually learns to adopt a realistic view of social aspects of life by learning to accept less-than-ideal end points.

"Looking back, I know there are times when I've been too involved in my children's social situations."

As you assist your child in looking beyond today, you might want to share with him this parent's story:

"When my son was in sixth grade, I bought him one pair of expensive white shoes for two sports. He had to wear the same shoes for soccer and baseball.

"The kids made fun of him. They called him "Whiteshoes." He was the only one with white shoes. I encouraged him to go along with the teasing and reminded him it wasn't the end of the world: he had good shoes and was able to play both sports.

"The next year, Whiteshoes was still his nickname even though he had outgrown those shoes. Now, it worked to his advantage. When his teammates called plays for Whiteshoes, the other team didn't know who that was!"

Identify the Depth of Your Involvement

Dealing with social development is not only difficult for a child; it can also be difficult for a parent. For example, I love to know all about my children's friends. I love to talk with the parents of my children's friends. Looking back, I know there are times when I've been too involved in their social situations.

What about you: Do you tend to be too directive? Too protective? Too loose?

Neither you nor I should take away our child's choices of friends. Neither you nor I should limit our child's friendships by social class, race, or sex. That would be wrong.

However, many parents believe they should intervene if a tweenager's friends negatively influence their child. Your degree of involvement is a judgment call. What you do will reflect your personal style. Your level of involvement should most clearly reflect your child's development, the amount of experience your child has had with a variety of social situations, the types of judgment calls he has made in the past, and your personal comfort level. Consider all of these aspects to determine if and how you will directly impact a social situation.

Here's how one parent wrestled with these issues: "When my son had his eighth birthday, we had a slumber party. He invited eight little boys I didn't know. That gave me a funny feeling; I didn't know their backgrounds. But I'll never refuse a child coming into my house. I'm more cautious when I allow my son to play at another child's house."

Some parents will naturally assume a more active role in their child's social experience than other parents. There are few strict guidelines, but I want to give you two specific suggestions:

Protect your child when necessary. Here's one parent's experience: "The parents of my son's friend are going through a separation. Several times, the dad has beat the family car with a baseball bat. That's not the kind of environment I want my son playing in. Ben invites his friend to play at our house."

Sometimes, these decisions are defined by a time span or a particular incident. When that happens, be flexible enough to reconsider whether the course of action you have been following is still the right one. For example, in the situation noted before, after a peaceful period of family life, it might again be safe to allow Ben to play at his friend's house. The parent would need to be alert to this possibility.

Social experiences will follow the up-and-down pattern of a roller coaster during the tweenage years.

Respect your child's social world. Social experiences will follow the up-and-down pattern of a roller coaster during these years. Support from a distance, but avoid imposing yourself in day-to-day situations. A junior high school principal addressed this subject very effectively:

"Friendships go back and forth. One day kids will be best of buddies, then they'll have a little disagreement, and they'll tie up with other kids. Then they'll be real catty about their former friends, the ones they were with just yesterday! When parents get involved, the kids are back together as friends and the parents are still fighting with each other."

He advises, "Your child can probably deal with his own social problem. Don't get so emotionally involved yourself that you create more problems."

"Your child can probably deal with his own social problem. Don't get so emotionally involved yourself that you create more problems."

Your child will need to learn basic social competencies during this time. He will look to you for help.

Support the Development of Social Skills

"There's a recurring social problem at this age," said a veteran educator. "A student wants to be part of the group but doesn't have the social graces to be accepted."

You can't force others to like your child. But you can help your child develop the skills he needs to be accepted. He will use the skills he learns right now for the rest of his life. Your child should be building the kinds of social skills listed in figure 4.1.

What can happen when these social skills aren't learned? A junior high teacher described a bright student who had trouble making any friends. "Every year, he slipped and slipped until he hung around troublemakers. I know he is very smart. He could be so successful. But he withdrew his own potential just so he could fit into a group and be accepted. He didn't know any other way to make friends."

You can't force others to like your child, but you can help your child develop the skills he needs to be accepted.

This was a tragedy that didn't need to happen. By helping your child learn social skills, you will be giving your child the tools he needs to be able to function in his broadening social world. How effectively he uses those skills will be increasingly obvious as you hear him talk about school.

Your child might say this:	Social skill your child can learn/practice	How you can support the skill development	Indication that child is developing the skill:
"Nobody likes me." "Everybody hates me."	Distinguish between what's real and what's perceived.	Ask your child, "What makes you say that? How do you know?" Help him see the difference between what is really happening and what he thinks might be happening. If your child actually doesn't have any friends, help him identify one person to whom he could speak and how he could approach the person. For example, you might ask: "You sit next to Brad on the school bus. What could you talk about tomorrow?"	"Chad didn't like me today because I wouldn't play basketball. I told him I'd play tomorrow."
"I had a fight with Erin, today. She says I can't talk to Colleen because I'm supposed to be *her* best friend."	Learn various levels and definitions for friendship.	Ask: "What does 'best friend' mean to Erin? What does 'best friend' mean to you?" Help her see how definitions can vary. Encourage her to discuss this with friends and come to a solution. Help her understand that friends can disagree and still be friends.	"Erin and I will be over at Colleen's house."
"When I'm with Courtney, everything's fine. When I'm with Kara and Courtney, they ignore me."	Practice problem solving in social settings.	Help her identify possible reasons she is excluded. Then ask, "What can you do to solve the problem?" Also remind her that friends might go through moody times, just like she does.	"Friends are worth having." "I like having friends."
"Nobody picked me for a partner, so I got stuck with Jason."	Plan social strategy for future use.	Acknowledge that this kind of situation happens sometimes. Help your child identify a plan that might prevent this from happening next time. You might say, "Next time, to whom can you talk before P.E. so you can set up a partner, in advance?"	"Chad was my partner in P.E. today."

Figure 4.1

Your Role in School Socialization

Many of the social dilemmas your child faces during this time period will be school related. Although you will not be observing these situations firsthand, you still have an important role. In the following example, you'll see how a parent listened, supported, and then used the situation as a springboard to broaden a sixth grader's understanding of friendship.

"Somebody wrote 'Jamie and Josh' on Jamie's backpack. Jamie was really embarrassed, but I told her I couldn't buy her a new backpack so she would need to get along with what she had. Jamie came up with the idea of painting a design over the pocket where the writing was. Actually seeing her name matched up with a single boy resulted in her saying, 'I don't think I want to have another boyfriend for a while.' We talked, then, about how it's nice to be friends with a lot of people."

This parent demonstrated support as Jamie worked through the problem. Because of her mom's approach, Jamie will probably be willing to come to her parent for help in the future.

Many school social situations will be set up as competitions: your child will compete directly against peers for a trophy or a prize. Whenever possible provide neutral or cooperative situations with these same children. Encourage teamwork. Affirm partnership. Support cooperation. Social interaction is encouraged when your child moves with others toward a common goal. The kitchen might be a mess after three ten year olds make trail mix to take on the science club hike, but your child will have memories of a wonderful social experience.

You might need to work in partnership with your child's teacher or school personnel to help resolve socially-based problems. Sometimes peer situations affect a child's school performance. You might also ask for assistance at school if such problems impact your child's emotional health or normal sleeping or eating patterns. Here's one example from a school principal:

"The parents of a really bright boy came in for a conference. He was a normal, great kid, but they were concerned that he didn't have any friends. I told the parents what he was doing in class to get the negative attention of his peers: picking his nose, losing his place when called on for an answer, being mean to kids in his high performance group.

"Then, we brought in the student. We talked about his strengths and how he could build on them. We reviewed what he was doing in class. We couldn't get him friends immediately, but over the year he developed them."

These parents needed to offer long-term support to their son. Part of this support was becoming aware of situations in which he could develop and practice social skills.

Be alert to natural opportunities to increase social skills. Many kinds of social situations offer the potential for your child's social development. During these years, your child will be involved in many spontaneous incidents with peers you'll never even know about. But at other times, help your child seize the moment for social growth. Your child can develop skills by interacting with people of all ages, in a variety of settings.

One junior high school principal has set up a program where students regularly relate to residents of a local nursing home. He says, "Kids need to be in situations where they respond to adults and aren't just herded around by a Scout leader. Kids need actual interaction where they look an adult in the eye, listen, and explain their feelings. This kind of social practice with adults will transfer to situations with peers." Attending a family reunion or spending a day on the job with you can offer your child similar opportunities.

During these years, encourage your child to develop friendships with a coach, a neighbor, or even the parent of a peer. You might invite your child's teachers or coaching staff to your home for dinner, or wait the extra five minutes so your child can talk to the youth worker after church. Being comfortable with people of all ages can boost your child's confidence as she develops relationships with those people who are so important to her, her peers.

Being comfortable with people of all ages can boost your child's confidence as she develops relationships with those people who are so important to her, her peers.

Two major changes in our society will affect these types of socialization opportunities:

- the increasing number of latchkey children, kids who come home to an empty house after school
- the increasing number of organized after-school activities

As a result, the traditional after-school invitation, "Come over and play," is heard less frequently. This implies that you will need to be very sensitive to your child's need for informal socialization that, in previous generations, was naturally built into the schedule.

And what about that eleven year old who is happier by himself than with others? Or that nine year old who, as one mother says, "would rather stay home and read a book than ride bikes with the kids down the street."

Some children are by nature not as social as others. Not every child should be a leader, highly talkative, or the life of the fifth grade Valentine's Day party. Developmentally, children during this time can be moody, and there are times when they really want to be alone. That need must be respected.

Patterns of friendship often emerge during these years: Some children want a "best friend"; others have many acquaintances. There is no "correct" number of friendships; there is no "right" depth to peer relationships. Each child, however, should be supported in his efforts to relate to others.

Avoid the Setup: Peers vs. Family

When your child is eight, nine, or ten, your family will still be his social center. He strongly identifies with you and what you do. When your child becomes eleven or twelve, you'll see signs of the shift we've discussed: what his friends think and say will become increasingly important.

I've seen this happen with our son, Matthew. Before this transition, shopping for school clothes was never a major expedition. Although Matthew has always preferred the color green and liked some styles more than others, we never spent very long in the boys' clothing department. He would hurriedly try on what we picked and then we were done.

Shopping with "Matthew the Tweenager" was a totally different experience. First, he was eager to go to the mall. That amused and confounded his sisters, who remembered him complaining about buying clothes. There were other major differences, too. It took so long that I thought we'd never get done! Matthew walked around every single clothes rack before even choosing what to take to the fitting room. He was concerned about making the "right" decision. His choices weren't based on my preferences, however. Matthew chose the kind of shirt his friend wears instead of the shirt I preferred because he could wear it to church and school.

You are certainly not "losing" your child. He is carrying the social skills and values you have taught him into wider social circles where others will influence him and test those standards.

What happened? His social base shifted from our family to his friends. You will see this happen with your child when you shop for clothes or plan family activities. You'll see it reflected in the way your child spends his leisure time. This does not mean, as one parent has said, "His friends have won and I have lost." No! This is natural and should be expected. But you are certainly not "losing" your child. He is carrying the social skills and values you have taught him into wider social circles where others will influence him and test those standards.

Wrap-Up

Helping your tweenager negotiate the maze of social situations may be one of the greatest challenges you ever face as a parent. But it's also a wonderful opportunity. You continue to have an important role in your child's social development, even though your child's friends, school personnel, other family members, and peers are influencing him to a greater degree than they did before. Your role in your child's social development can't be overemphasized. As one school psychologist said, "The child who is able to get along with at least his own small group, who has a good friend or friends, is more emotionally, physically, and cognitively secure."

During these years, your child has the first opportunity to develop and maintain long-term friendships that are outside your neighborhood and family circle. Your child is building onto the foundation of social skills you helped to shape.

Hosting a sleep over, driving five miles to pick up your child's friend, or inviting your child's classmate for dinner won't guarantee your child will win a popularity contest. But your support in the social arena will impact all areas of your child's development.

Chapter 5

Emotional Development:
Learning Self-Esteem

The following statements are basic facts.

- Feelings are neither good nor bad.
- Feelings affect behavior.
- Feelings cannot be learned by direct teaching.
- The way your child feels about himself impacts all other aspects of life.
- Your child needs a sense of security.
- Your child needs to know he is loved, accepted, and appreciated.

Emotional needs don't change through the years. But during the years from eight to twelve, there are some dramatic changes in how you will help your child deal with emotions and how you express emotions to him. Your preteen might also be more aware than she was in the past of her many and conflicting feelings, perceptions, and interpretations.

I remember how Christy, as a preschooler, wanted to hold onto me forever. As a sixth grader, she didn't always want to be seen with me! However, Christy, like your tweenager, still needed love from her parents.

You will welcome some signs of emotional development. For example, your eight or nine year old can understand how someone else feels if he has had a similar experience. If a friend's grandfather dies, your son will be able to say, with great understanding, "I heard your grandpa died. I'm really sorry. I was mad when my grandma died."

By the age of ten or twelve, your child will be able to actually understand your viewpoint. As he becomes less self-centered, he will be able to see why you are upset that Aunt Eva wants to bring her pesky dog that yaps continually for Thanksgiving Day dinner. Even if your child has not experienced exactly the same feelings you have, he will be able to see a situation from your point of view.

"Dad, I'm too old to have a baby-sitter."

Your child will become emotionally less dependent. That means you can run next door to deliver a plate of fresh cookies for an ill neighbor and leave your child alone for a couple of minutes. The flip side of this growing independence is that you might face some awkward transitions. For example, a nine year old might say, "Dad, I'm too old to have a baby-sitter." You can remind him, "But you don't like to be alone after it gets dark outside." Your child might want to feel independent but might not be quite ready to be independent. Children in this age range are becoming more emotionally grown-up, but they won't cut the home ties just yet.

Your child might want to *feel* independent but might not be quite ready to *be* independent.

MIRROR TALK

I knew my child was changing emotionally, when _____
_____.

*When I was about my child's age, one person who was emotionally supportive to me was*_____
_____.

I know my child felt good about herself when _____
_____.

How can you give your child a lifelong lift toward a positive self concept? How can you support your child's move toward emotional independence? It's important to begin by understanding your own strengths and nurturing your own self-esteem.

Understand Your Own Strengths

Dealing with some aspects of emotional development will challenge every single ounce of parenting strength you have. As one mother remembered, "The hardest time for me as a parent was when my daughter was around eight and a half. We were at odds, constantly. And it seemed to happen all of a sudden one day. When Langley left for school that morning, I was the most wonderful mother in the world. When she came home, I wasn't worth a piece of dirt."

Dealing with some aspects of emotional development will challenge every single ounce of parenting strength you have.

This mom clearly identified the situation many parents face. As one school psychologist told me, "What causes parents the most trouble is the basic nature of the developing child. Their behavior is very erratic. The child can be happy one moment and feel the world is a horrible place in just the next minute."

If this happens to you, remember that your child is going through major changes. Her social world is being turned upside down, sometimes on a daily basis. Girls, especially, are undergoing dramatic hormonal shifts. Even school, which can be such a steady element through the years for boys and girls, is different from what it was in the past. Your child's emotional shifts during this time might give you new understanding of the term *tough love.*

But remembering all those important facts won't change the way you feel. Be aware of your own emotional state during this time. Your child's mood swings and changeable tone can trigger some strong feelings inside you.

"All of the sudden, I was the bad guy. I was off limits. She was insulted if I even said 'Hello' to her friends."

As one parent said, "I had put so much time and energy into her for ten years. All of the sudden, I was the bad guy. I was off limits. She was insulted if I even said 'Hello' to her friends. My son went through the same thing. Beginning in about the middle of sixth grade, he was too cool for his own family."

You might experience these problems to a greater or lesser extent. But at some point, your child's emotional development will probably force you into dealing with some intense emotions.

MIRROR
TALK

How would I feel if my child told me, "Mom, just drop me off a block away from school today. I don't want my friends to see you in our old car"?___

How will I maintain a personally strong self-concept as a parent, during these potentially unsettling years?___

How can I feel good about my parenting when my child doesn't feel good about me?___

What are three strengths I bring to parenting?___

Anticipate how you might deal with your child. And since the "Daddy, I love you" notes will quite possibly stop for a while, identify in advance sources of affirmation for yourself during this time.

You are bringing significant strengths to your parenting at this time. You have nurtured your child for many years. You have learned about your child. You have learned about yourself. Use this knowledge and apply the skills you've learned so that these years will be a time of personal development for you and continued growth for your child.

Feeling good about yourself is the first step toward helping your child feel good about himself.

Nurture Self-Esteem

"Our daughter wasn't quite eight yet. Lindsey was very tall, though, and had below average self-esteem because of that. She was quiet and hung on me a lot. At school, they tested for the gifted class. Lindsey didn't get into that, and her friends did.

"She was on a local swim team, and that summer, the coach really encouraged her to work. Lindsey was physically built to be a good swimmer, and she applied herself. She worked hard, swimming two practices a day.

"In regional competition, Lindsey did very well. She placed first in all four of her events. They had an Olympic-like, pyramid stand for the winners.

"When she was up there on that stand, I could tell she had grown inwardly and was feeling good about herself.

"From that day on, Lindsey excelled. That experience made a real difference in how Lindsey related to peers, how she did at school, and how she related to teachers. She had to work very hard, but she applied herself.

"Last year, Lindsey had to write an essay for a college entrance application. She told the story about that day on the winner's platform when she felt so good about herself."

This mother says both she and Lindsey feel this single incident contributed to Lindsey's development of a positive self-concept, feeling good about herself. By winning those races, Lindsey looked not only at who she was but at the person she wanted to become. Living up to her expectations, and perhaps those of her coach and mother, contributed to her overall sense of self-worth. Lindsey didn't know it, but those internal comparisons and the meeting of expectations contributed to building a high self-esteem. What Lindsey experienced, is, developmentally, what you can anticipate will happen to your child during this age span.

Some Guidelines

Timing was important for Lindsey. Beginning at about age seven, children don't just think about who they are, they broaden their outlook to include "the ideal me." That's why helping a child develop a sense of vision and supporting a "be whatever you want to be" view of the future had such a major impact on Lindsey. This approach can also impact your child. You cannot give your child self-esteem, but you can directly contribute to the development of a positive self-concept. Here are five guidelines:

Accept your child's feelings. Those feelings are valid. Avoid comments that might result in your child repressing his emotions. For example, saying something like, "Now don't get upset if Jason gets the lead in the play," might indicate that your child shouldn't share his real feelings. Your child might get the idea that he should tell you about only emotions you will like. Share your perspective on a situation, but don't write off the way he feels. Give your child permission to experience a normal range of emotions.

By this time, though, your child should know the proper place and time to share feelings. For example, when your child was younger, he might have told Aunt Emma, "I don't like your pickled watermelon." Now, instead of expressing that sentiment while seated at a family dinner, your child will share his feelings in a private moment with you.

Acknowledge your child's attempts, not just his successes. Your child should have many opportunities to try a variety of activities. As one parent said, "Kids needs lots of chances to shine. When they have a chance to try water polo and tap dancing and piano, they have lots of opportunities to emerge as leaders. Let them have a little taste just so they hear the applause for something they've done."

You might let your child sign up for a craft class at the local park. Later in the year, he might start swimming lessons at the local YMCA. Or you might drive him to church every Saturday to practice volleyball with the youth team. Encourage him to sample from a smorgasbord of experiences. Then provide the support he needs.

Be aware that your child will feel the ever-increasing pull of peer influence in this phase of life. As one parent observed, "The kids started grouping and labeling, all on their own. They were always saying, 'He's the artist,' or 'She can run.'" If you notice this happening to your child, help her consider many personal options before peer pressure limits the possibilities.

Be a positive role model. My children easily pinpoint my shortcomings; I need to remind them, occasionally, of my strengths! Be honest with your children about who you are and what you can do.

Show your child how to learn from failure. A new twist on a familiar saying is correct: "Experience isn't the best teacher. Learning from experience is the best teacher." Your child's self-esteem will grow when she learns this fact.

Be honest with your praise. Helping your child build a positive self-image doesn't imply that you must clap enthusiastically when your child squeaks his violin or falls from the beam during a gymnastics meet. In any situation, going overboard with lavish congratulations will reduce the credibility of your honest praise. Your applause will make a positive contribution when your child knows he has done something to earn it. Match your expression of appreciation to the level of achievement.

Preadolescence is a time when self-esteem can sink to new lows. Your child will be very aware of his mistakes and his perceived shortcomings. You have the position and the opportunity to help him continue to build a healthy self-concept.

Build a Sense of Worth Through Responsibility

Your child needs to feel he has an important place in your family. One of the easiest and most effective ways to communicate this concept is to give your child responsibilities. Gradually increase the number or alter the type of chores your child does as she moves through these years.

The parent of one eight year old told me, "We built self-esteem by dealing with personal responsibilities. We started with little issues like returning library books on time, remembering to change underwear, and having his shower done by 8:30 each night."

Periodically, review what your child does around the house. Then consider what he might be capable of doing. Conduct your review at specific times during the calendar year. In our family, we do this each summer before we walk into the house after our vacation trip. We discuss what new responsibilities each child will assume. We talk about what they will need to learn in order to be successful with their new chore. My husband and I clarify who will teach them the new job skills. You might do this same thing at your child's next birthday. Perhaps your child gives the guinea pig food and water every day. Now she might be ready to learn how to clean out the cage.

As you consider building self-esteem through various

household responsibilities, keep in mind these four suggestions:

Teach your child. At the age of eight, nine, or ten, children do not automatically know how to vacuum a rug or scour a sink. You will need to teach such jobs. Invest time and energy in this process: you are not only telling about procedures, but you are communicating your expectations and standards. Be patient: she might not meet your standards the first time.

Rotate jobs. Since a major goal is to help your child feel good about how he is joyfully contributing to the family, you'll want to ensure pleasant working conditions. Any job can get boring, so vary responsibilities. For example, during one month your child might clear the table after supper and the following month do the same job after breakfast instead.

Avoid the temptation to add jobs as your child gets older. A list of chores can become impossibly long. Instead, substitute more complicated jobs for simpler jobs. For example, as an eight year old, your son might have been responsible for shoveling snow off the front porch. As a ten year old, he might clean snow off the car and scrape the windshield instead.

Support your child's follow-through. He might need reminders to do his job. But since you want him to gain a sense of responsibility, communicate reminders in ways which encourage him to accept the responsibility. For example, instead of continually saying, "Take out the garbage," post a checklist on the refrigerator. Then, he can independently track his progress.

In some ways, you might regard assigning chores as a way for a child to "earn his keep." But this issue has far more meaning. By contributing to the family, your child sees how he has his own meaningful niche.

One mother of an eight year old and fifteen year old said, "This stage is a mixed blessing. We all like to be needed. That's being a mom, isn't it? I miss it. But it's so neat to see a new level of responsibility being achieved because it does so much for the child." And that, after all, is the bottom line as we help a child feel a sense of worth and value.

I started this chapter by saying emotional needs don't change, but the ways we meet those needs change. You've seen that truth demonstrated during this discussion about self-concept. You'll also see this, perhaps more dramatically, as you express love to your preteen.

Demonstrate Your Love

The same child who as a five year old eagerly reached up to kiss you good-bye when the school bus came now might kiss you only at bedtime; even then, he might hesitate. It's not that your child doesn't love you anymore. He's just searching for age-appropriate ways to express that emotion.

MIRROR
TALK

My child likes to be hugged when _____

_____.

I know my child loves me because _____

_____.

*Most of the time, I show my child, "I love you" when*_____

_____.

Your child might have difficulty both expressing and receiving your love during these years. As one mother said, "We went through a rough time in fifth and sixth grade when our daughter wasn't physical with us. It wasn't cool to kiss a mom, but Lisa still needed those hugs. So did I."

"It wasn't cool to kiss a mom, but Lisa still needed those hugs. So did I."

Be sensitive to the time and place you choose to physically express your love to your child. You might skip the hug when you drop your child off for a church youth outing and substitute an "I'm glad your home" hug in the living room when your child returns home.

You might leave a note on your child's pillow or desk. Or mail your child a "thinking of you" card—even eleven year olds like to get mail! Also encourage brothers and sisters, grandparents, and other relatives to continue to express love to your preadolescent in appropriate ways.

Wrap-Up

Coping with the emotional side of your child's development is a constant challenge during these years. You might find it helpful to remember that other parents are living with their child's mood swings and erratic behavior, too.

One school psychologist admitted, "The emotional upheaval makes this an exhausting time to parent. The very unpredictability is the hardest thing to deal with. You always have to be prepared for anything."

In an ideal world, the simple act of giving love would be enough to foster a child's healthy emotional development. It would be easy to hug away, forever, the hurt for a child who lost the spelling bee. A kiss would completely console the ten year old track star who tripped just in front of the finish line. But in the real world of parenting, you will need to continually seek ways to foster healthy emotional development of your preteen. Even then, there are no guarantees. There isn't a magic formula to build self-esteem, self-worth, or feelings of competence, but now you have knowledge to build on. As you are challenged in this area, perhaps these words from a parent of three will give you some encouragement: "Don't give up on your kids. Every parent hits a lot of roadblocks at this time, but you can do it."

Chapter 6

Spiritual Development:
Growing Up with God

Spiritual development has been described as the most
difficult area in which to parent. In some ways, I agree with
that. I can easily measure my children's physical growth
with a yardstick, judge their social development with how
they relate to others when I drive the car pool, and even
evaluate emotional growth when I observe how they handle grades on tests. But because spiritual growth doesn't fit
into a neat little package, it's harder for me to get a handle
on how my children are growing with God.

Perhaps you, too, find this area very challenging. If so,
you might have felt or said:

- "I don't have all the answers to complex questions
  about faith, death, and eternal life. When my kid
  asks about these things, I feel stupid."

- "Talking about my faith reflects a very personal relationship. It's embarrassing to talk about this to my son."
- "My child is asking the same questions I'm asking. I can't help him come to terms with issues like, 'Why does God let good people suffer?' if I'm looking for an answer to the same question."
- "I don't know what to do now: My ten year old knows all the Bible stories. What's next?"

Some parents struggle with grudges against the church in which they were raised. They feel unsettled and uncomfortable when they see a child dealing with the same issues they've never settled for themselves. Other parents, who did not grow up in a Christian home, do not have a model of spiritual nurturing.

Parents feel unsettled and uncomfortable when they see a child dealing with the same issues they've never settled for themselves.

MIRROR
TALK

*When do you feel closest to God?*_____

_____

*When did you last hear God's voice?*_____

_____

*How do you mentally picture God?*_____

_____

(Ask your child these questions, too.)
*What did you say to your child recently that reflected your belief in God?*____

_____

You have a critical role as a spiritual educator. Spiritual development takes place against the backdrop of your family's religious experience. Devotions, mealtime prayers, and the celebration of Christian traditions can directly impact a child's spiritual journey. Church participation gives a framework in which a child practices his beliefs.

As your child moves through these years, you will probably confirm what noted Harvard professor Robert Coles observed: Your child's moral life overlaps with his religious life; his religious life overlaps his spiritual life.[1]

"My own personal morality influences to a great extent the kinds of things I do as a parent."

As you observe this dynamic in your child's life, you might discover the same thing is true in your own life. As a parent of two told me so eloquently, "My own personal morality influences to a great extent the kinds of things I do as a parent. God has given me my children. As a steward, it's my responsibility to do the very best I can, with His help. It's the Christian lifestyle which helps me define areas in which I can determine, 'This is right. This is wrong.'"

Your child's spiritual development will not follow a straight line. You will see peaks and valleys.

As is true in other areas, your child's spiritual development will not follow a straight line. You will see peaks and valleys as your child might alternately accept and then question God's love. You will begin to see your child reflect his maturing spirituality in new and different ways.

Here are seven developmental characteristics that will affect how you encourage your preadolescent to grow up with God:

Helping Others

Because your child can now empathize, or feel with and for people, he is interested in the well-being of others. Here's an example from a teacher: "We were talking about writing letters to the president. When we talked about what problems he should address, the children brought up subjects of rape, the homeless, AIDS, and other topics I would not bring up in our fourth grade classroom. One little boy was extremely concerned and said with great feeling, 'We've got to do something about these problems.' It was mind-boggling how much the children knew about the issues and how much they wanted to help."

Give your child appropriate opportunities to assist others. In most cases, your child will most easily identify with mission oriented projects close to home instead of those with a global scope or a far-off location. For example, one family signed up to deliver gifts to local families during a holiday sharing program. The mother said, "My kids were stunned at the poverty in which people live so close to our house. Our kids felt that delivering a car full of clothing and toys wasn't enough." Each December, our children make gifts and cards to deliver to homebound members of our church. Two of our children regularly accompany my husband on visits to shut-in members.

Your nine year old might want to host a lemonade stand at a garage sale and donate her profits to a local shelter for abused children. Your ten year old might want to participate in a jump rope marathon to raise money for a community center. Your twelve year old might want to attend a weekend work camp. These are all appropriate ways for your child to act out his Christian concern for others.

A New View of the Bible

When your child was younger, she focused on favorite parts and characters in Bible stories. Now, she wants to know how Bible stories relate to her. She learns these things most easily in a class setting. Here's an example:

A fifth and sixth grade class acted out a modern-day version of the parable of the good Samaritan. They depicted unlikely heroes helping a nerd lying hurt on the side of the road. (The nerd cried out, 'Help! I've fallen and I can't get up!') They showed kids responding compassionately to a football player who ran the wrong way for a touchdown. Most of all, they showed that they understood what Jesus meant when he said to be a good neighbor.[2]

This type of focused learning situation seldom occurs in family settings unless it is structured as part of a family devotion. But it's important to understand why your child brings home relational Bible study booklets or faith-application papers instead of the leaflets he carried home in previous years.

Also, you can be alert to opportunities at home for your child to take a Bible truth to a new level with your own "faith in action" step: For example, a nine year old who sees you write a check to put in the offering will see you practice stewardship. When he asks, "How much do you give?" you'll have an opportunity to talk about your tithing and his giving. An eleven year old who overhears you inviting a neighbor to an Easter worship service will see how you interpret the Great Commission of Matthew 28:19–20. When your son asks, "Weren't you embarrassed?" the door is open for you to discuss evangelism with him.

In these two examples, it would not be enough for the parent to simply write the offering check or invite the neighbor to church. The parent needs to go one step further if the child is going to benefit. The parent needs to connect his action to his faith.

Questions

For preadolescents, talking about religious issues usually includes raising questions. The blind acceptance of earlier years will be replaced by a search for facts. Although some parents panic at this point, it's better to offer guidance and patience.

Avoid viewing your child's questions as a sign of rebellion; see them instead as an opportunity for teaching. When your child asks a question, he is seeking an answer. Help him in his search.

Avoid viewing your child's questions as a sign of rebellion; see them instead as an opportunity for teaching.

More than ever before, your family will need to be a spiritual sanctuary where your child can find security even though he might struggle with personal doubts about God. Your child needs to know that even if he raises concerns, you and God will still love him. It's important for him to enter his teen years sure of that fact.

MIRROR
TALK

When I was my child's age, I remember thinking that God_____

_____.

When my child asks questions about God, I feel_____

_____.

One way I can help my child in his spiritual journey is_____

_____.

Setting a tone of certainty in God's faithfulness is easiest if you regularly read the Bible, pray, and have devotions. A parent who continues his own spiritual journey models assurance of faith in ways that can impact even the most skeptical tweenager.

Because your child has a somewhat questioning attitude during this time, he'll be extremely alert to inconsistencies in your own faith. If you knowingly keep the extra dollar the store clerk mistakenly handed you, your child will be the first one to notice. Your child will readily expand upon such seemingly insignificant hypocritical behaviors or remarks. You'll want to live out the words in Deuteronomy 11:19: "You shall teach them to your children, speaking of them when you sit in your house, when you walk by the way, when you lie down, and when you rise up" (NKJV).

As your child begins to test her knowledge of God against the background of broadened personal experiences, she will need a version of the Bible with which she can feel comfortable. Your child is most likely to use her Bible if she has helped pick it out. Encourage your child to choose a translation, binding, and format she likes. You will probably see individual differences reflected in your children's choices. When our son, Matthew, was eight, he chose a Bible that had the best picture of David and Goliath, his favorite Bible story. Angie was nine and a half years old when she chose a Bible with a denim cover. Christy picked a Bible with study aids and maps. Christy was the only one of our children who even considered the type of language used in the translation.

Faith Awareness

As your child raises questions and grows in spiritual knowledge, he will have an increased awareness of the awesome nature of faith. For some preteens, walking with God can appear overwhelming and even scary. If your child shares these kinds of feelings, you can help him in two ways.

For some preteens, walking with God can appear overwhelming and even scary.

First, remember aloud with your child the time you were his age. Your "I remember when" statement probably won't generate the "Oh no, Mom," response you might get when discussing clothing trends. Spiritual issues cut across the years; they aren't culturally shaped like how far kids walk to school or how much they earn on their first job. Your child will probably listen if you talk about your own junior high struggles with religion.

Second, support your child's involvement with a church youth group. Preteens want to belong. Youth ministry events will offer your child an opportunity to relate with others who are dealing with the same type of questions your child is asking. In addition, youth ministers generally gear study and discussion sessions to answer common questions. So encourage but don't pressure your child to participate.

At the same time, you might offer to drive the group to a nursing home, take a two-hour shift during an all-night lock-in, or assist with a Saturday morning pancake breakfast. You might volunteer to host church meetings or provide refreshments. Because some preteens are starting to feel a need to distance themselves from parents in peer situations, check with your child first to see how she'd like you to help. Offer your support and then wait for her response.

Spiritual Anchors

Family traditions offer a sense of stability for a preadolescent who is dealing with change in every area of life. A spiritually focused ritual or event can also give a sense of structure and identity, even as your child is raising basic questions about his relationship to God.

MIRROR
TALK

I feel church attendance is _____
_____.

My child feels church attendance is _____
_____.

I support my child's participation in church events by _____
_____.

At this time in life, your child will appreciate traditions that aren't seen as babyish. If you are sensitive and responsive to these concerns, your child can continue to grow spiritually through everyday traditions and special day celebrations.

For example, "Do I have to go?" is a typical way in

which your tweenager might question the tradition of attending church regularly. Your child will be most likely to raise this issue if worship attendance is viewed as an obligation instead of an opportunity. When your child was younger you simply stated, "You must go to church because that's what you must do." That was appropriate for a six year old. Now, you can discuss worship attendance in a way that will encourage your preteen to use his new thinking abilities and make some judgments about religion in his own life. You might talk with your child about how you view worship: as an opportunity to thank God for His blessings, to be reminded of His continued faithfulness, and to receive renewed strength for a daily walk with Him, for example.

Preteens will attend church most readily under one or more of the following conditions.

They participate. They might be involved as a greeter, an acolyte, a reader, a choir member, or in a variety of other ways. Involvement capitalizes on your child's desire to serve and offers a built-in way to "fit in."

They make a choice. Most churches offer several worship options. When you encourage your child to attend the service at the time and in the format she prefers, you are recognizing her growing independence and ability to make wise decisions. We've used this approach in our family so that our children's choice isn't "Should I go to church or should I stay home?" but "Which service should I attend?"

They have friends who also attend. Socialization is a major part of a preteen's life. Seeing friends at church can be part of what your child values about attending. Remember, every situation, including going to church, has the appeal and attraction of becoming a social experience for your child. Our son had renewed enthusiasm for attending

Sunday school when his age finally made him eligible to play Christian Nintendo games in the youth room with friends.

Your Influence

As you see your eleven year old passionately caring for God's world through environmental issues or your twelve year old choosing among varied church activities, you might uncover new opportunities for your own spiritual growth. One mom said, "For two years, I attended my husband's Bible class. Then we started a mini-Bible class at church for children to give them a good understanding of the Bible. Now I'm in a Bible study with my twelve year old, and he's questioning the whole area of commitment to Christ. For my own relating of faith to my children, I am more comfortable and confident when I'm in an ongoing discussion group or Bible study."

As this parent discovered, a preadolescent isn't the only one who might grow spiritually during these years.

You might discover in a totally new way what this classic statement means: God uses other people to help you grow with Him. God might use your child to help you, a parent of a tweenager. Consider a thoughtful answer when your nine year old asks, "Daddy, why don't you go to church with us?" Respond from the heart when your eight year old asks, "Mommy, will you come to church and see me in the Christmas program?" Allow yourself to be open to God working through your child, and you might grow in ways you never anticipated.

And as you continue to grow spiritually, you will impact your child's spiritual development. How you come to terms with God in your personal relationship with Him, the ways in which you rationalize not attending church, or the joy-filled service you give as a Bible study leader will personalize the perspective your child develops about the faith-life connection. Talking with your child about faith challenges communicates, "You're not the only one; I struggle too." Whenever possible, share these issues in the context that you, too, are still growing with God. By doing this, you will communicate to your child that spiritual development is lifelong.

Your child will form her own view of God.

However, remember that your child will form her own view of God. She will look for Him to be active in her life. She will build a personal relationship with Him. As much as you love your child, you cannot earn a place for her in heaven or give her the gift of faith. But be open to God's leading, and He will be faithful to you in your parenting.

Personal Religious Practices

Your preteen should be encouraged to continue to pray and have devotions; however, the way in which he participates in these activities will probably change in response to his new level of development.

Harvard scholar Robert Coles demonstrated that children, including preteens, are clearly eager and willing to talk about God. This fits a developmental characteristic that you see in your child: As a child grows he spends increasing amounts of time in conversation. Because prayer is defined as talking and listening to God, this is an ideal time to help your child grow through prayer.

In one family, the parent explained, "We don't use rote

prayers. We talk to God in our own words. A lot of times, now, Jeff will whisper his own prayers at night without me. If we pray together, he'll still do his own little thing, too."

"A lot of times, now, Jeff will whisper his own prayers at night without me."

At mealtime, you might use a circle prayer in which each person tells God one thing for which he is thankful. This practice allows your child to continue conversations with God even though he might be dealing with spiritual questions or doubts.

Or your child might adapt the journal writing experiences from school to keeping a prayer journal at home. You can jump-start your child to write down personal requests and to record God's responses by keeping a notebook to which everyone can contribute near the dinner table or in the family area. In this way, your preadolescent will not stand apart but will make a contribution to the family. You may develop any pattern for this kind of journal entry. One suggestion is to divide the notebook page into four columns labeled *date, request, thanksgiving,* and *requested by.*

Your child might prefer to have a private prayer diary. The writing done by tweenagers is sometimes more revealing than their speech, so your child might want to keep private his conversations with God. If so, respect this wish.

There are a few books of family devotions written to be appropriate for all ages. Such devotions include a Scripture selection, faith-related thoughts, and a prayer suggestion in a traditional format. However, your family may wish to reread Bible stories during family devotions now that your child is a preteen. She has new mental abilities. She is also bringing to Bible reading a broader background of life experience. For example, your twelve-year-old daughter will have a different understanding of Mary, the mother of Jesus, now that the unmarried teenager down the street from where you live is pregnant and just five years older than your daughter. Although the two situations are very different, your child will have a new perspective on the biblical character simply because of the personal experience with your neighbor.

Because your child might feel he's "too cool for God" and wants relevancy in his religious practices, some families choose to develop their own devotions instead of using printed resources. When your children are all older, you might read and discuss books by Madeleine L'Engle, Max Lucado, or C. S. Lewis. For example, after reading *The Chronicles of Narnia* our children had dinner table discussions about the parallels between their relationship to God and the Pevensie children's relationship to Aslan.

Your family might choose to create a totally new devotional format, designed to include your preteen. For example, during the week each person might look for signs of God's faithfulness or God's creativity, or God's forgiveness. Then individuals might share their findings during Saturday night supper.

Or you might allow preteens to select family devotional materials. When given this opportunity, your child might choose Christian music or videos. Be aware that, developmentally, few nine or ten year olds have the maturity to develop a meaningful devotion merely from a popular song. You will need to provide some structure to ensure that the devotion has spiritual impact. For example, your ten year old might select one particular song on a music video. Then the family can watch the selection, share what it means to them, and discuss how the message can have different meanings, how the format stifles or highlights the message, and whatever other issues that particular song presents.

These alternative devotional formats will not create the classic picture of a family gathered in the kitchen for a quiet time of reflection, but these varied experiences can have relevance. This is true not just for the preteen but for all family members who are emotionally open to various devotional styles.

In other homes, preteens are permitted to pull away completely from the family devotional scene. In this case, your child will need personal reading materials. When you and your child consider both fiction and nonfiction books, there will be a wide choice of materials from which to select (see Appendix B).

Reading Christian fiction is not the same as having a personal devotion. However, learning about others and their spiritual walks can have real meaning because your child will be continually looking for the relevance of God. Remember that your preteen now has the cognitive ability to transpose situations and empathize with others. It is not unusual for a twelve year old to relate human relationship issues of fictional characters to his real-life situations.

There are no clear-cut formulas to follow as your child begins to try out different formats for religious practices such as devotions. However, your child will continue to need your support and encouragement.

Wrap-Up

As your child grows from eight years old to twelve years old, your home will continue to be the best place for your child to grow up with God. Although this has been true since your child was a baby, it's especially important at this time. Your child is now seeking a personal relationship with God and internalizing his concept of God. There is no better place to grow in that relationship than in the comfort and security of another relationship, the family.

You will see your child take more steps forward than backward on his spiritual journey. Although your child might have moved beyond simply asking God for things he wants, he will continue to want immediate answers from Him. He will be capable of deeply religious feelings, but he still will not understand the many mysteries that can only be answered or accepted by those with a mature faith.

Your child will be capable of deeply religious feelings, but he still will not understand the many mysteries that can be answered or accepted by only those with a mature faith.

More than anything your child needs your continued prayers. Lift him up daily to God. And ask your child to pray for you, too. By sharing this aspect of the faith walk, you will grow in your relationship with each other and your individual relationships with God.

Part Two

Practical Parenting During the Preteen Years

Chapter 7

School Life

The major developmental changes that affect your child from eight to twelve are reflected in his world at school. The school schedule, environment, and experiences are designed specifically to respond to your child's new levels of development.

For example, as a result of your child's ability to give and take in a social situation, she might work in an assigned group during an entire school term. Because your child has a growing sense of time management skills and organizational techniques, he might be required to do a science fair project, due two months after the assignment is given. Because your child is developing more complex thinking skills, she might explore a single topic by using her abilities and knowledge in art, history, the language arts, and science. One parent described the school scene perfectly: "It's not cut it out, paste it on, and frame it, anymore. He has to think."

Children who zoomed to the top of the class during the primary years because of an enriched background and family life are seeing their initial gains level off. As one parent noticed, "Everybody else is starting to catch up to him now. He's not automatically at the top of the class."

Your child might experience some "firsts" at school including:

- Earning letter grades on a report card.
- Eating lunch with the "big kids."
- Having school permission to ride a bike.
- Using a locker.
- Becoming eligible for sports and school clubs.
- Earning a place on the honor roll.
- Receiving a detention for inappropriate behavior.
- Changing clothes for P.E.
- Being eligible for school leadership positions such as student council, safety patrol, lunch helper, hall monitor, and peer counselor.
- Surviving without recess.

Your child may be enrolled in an elementary school, a middle school, or a junior high school. As an eight to twelve year old, he is anywhere from a third grader to a seventh grader. He might spend five to eight hours in classes each day; additional time might be invested in school-sponsored activities. His school might be in session from August to May, September to June, or function on a year-round schedule.

But regardless of your child's age, no matter what the school is called, no matter the schedule, one thing is certain: you will still play a part in his life at school. At a minimum, you will support his work and develop a partnership with school personnel.

Your interest in school is extremely important. Research consistently underlines one fact: Children whose parents are involved in school will perform better in school. School achievement is unquestionably linked to parent participation. This is true at every grade level.

School, school friends, and school activities are the focal point for a tweenager. Here we'll discuss eleven specific ways you can help your child get the most benefit from these school years.

Be a Homework Helper

Homework is important. Through homework, your child will learn effective study skills and develop internal controls (or self-discipline). A teacher assigns homework to let students practice skills, to extend classroom learning, and to provide enrichment to school experiences.

Homework isn't new, for you or your child. You are already a veteran homework helper. In preschool, you sliced carrot sticks when it was your child's turn to bring the snack. In kindergarten, you carried the guinea pig to school for show-and-tell. In first grade, you listened as your child read aloud. In second grade, you helped review spelling words for tests each Friday.

At third or fourth grade, you'll notice a shift in teaching emphasis. Teachers will no longer devote the entire morning to reading and math. As a fourth grade teacher explained, "All of a sudden, social studies and science are on equal footing with reading, English, and math."

MIRROR
TALK

My child's favorite subject is _____

_____.

The most difficult subject for my child is _____

_____.

My child's favorite teacher this year is _____

_____.

The reason my child likes this teacher is _____

_____.

At third or fourth grade, depending on the instructional model used at your child's school, a somewhat dramatic shift in the approach to the structure of lessons will occur. As one parent told me, "All of a sudden, the teacher says, 'Here are the directions and here is when it's due. Now do it.'" That may be oversimplified, but there is definitely a new approach to instruction and assignments that will impact your child's homework.

"All of a sudden, the teacher says, 'Here are the directions and here is when it's due. Now do it.'"

You might need to assume an active role. One teacher advised, "Parents need to help. A parent shouldn't say, 'My responsibility is going to work. Your responsibility is doing your homework.' A fourth grader can't get through that by himself."

Your active participation decreases as your child moves toward eighth grade. You will notice a subtle shift around fifth grade; you'll know less about your child's actual assignments. You might occasionally review lists of material with your child when asked, but overall, you will become a support person instead of someone who interacts with your child and his assignments. Here are examples demonstrating how your homework involvement might change during these years:

- In third grade, you will save coffee cans for your child to roll across your kitchen floor so he can measure different speeds.
- In fourth grade, you will review with your child a list of states and their capitals.
- In fifth grade, you will take your child to the store each week so he can graph the prices of bread and lettuce.
- In sixth grade, you will point out Orion's Belt and the North Star as your child matches stars on his chart with what you see in the winter sky.
- In seventh grade, you will take your child to the library to use the encyclopedia.

If your child asks for assistance, begin by making sure he understands the assignment. Ask him to repeat the assignment to you, using his own words. If he's unsure about the basic nature of an assignment or is having problems and is frustrated, suggest these actions:

Reread the assignment. The instructions might be on a handout or in a textbook. After your child rereads the assignment, have her tell you what she thinks it means. If your child is unsure about the definition of a word in the assignment, encourage her to look up the meaning.

Phone a classmate. Keep a list of names and numbers by the telephone for this kind of peer counseling. Your child can and should learn to solve problems with the help of friends.

Consult other sources of information. Call a "homework hot line." In most cases, this is updated daily, and students or parents may phone to find out assignments. Or contact a friend or neighbor who had the same teacher in a previous school year.

If there is still a problem, encourage your child to complete all homework except the section about which there is a question. Then your child should plan to get to school before the usual time so that he can go to the classroom to talk with the teacher, leave a note in the teacher's mailbox, or request a pass to see the teacher during homeroom or lunch.

Resist the temptation to do your child's homework. A parent who does a child's homework cheats the child.

Occasionally your child may ask you to watch her work a problem or example. This is a good opportunity for your child to break down an assignment into smaller sections so the work isn't overwhelming. Your child might want to talk through the problem as she solves it. Observe quietly; then check the work, if possible. If there is an error, suggest that your child (not you) find and correct the problem. Praise her for a job well done.

Resist the temptation to do your child's homework. Your child is the learner. He will be evaluated on what he has learned. A parent who does a child's homework cheats the child. Avoid cheating your child. He deserves the opportunity to learn and achieve.

Help Your Child Establish a Routine

Study at home should be part of your child's regular routine. Some children do homework more efficiently if they play for a while after school and then begin chores and homework. Other children prefer getting homework done immediately after school. A child who comes home to an empty house might begin homework before you get home and mark questions or tough problems to discuss with you later.

Be especially patient with your eight or nine year old during the first year of "real" homework. He will need time and experience to discover his own most effective work patterns.

Children eight to twelve years old look for routines to give them a sense of stability and structure. A homework pattern can be one of these foundation points since your child will probably have homework on a regular basis. Third graders might have twenty minutes of work each week night. Beginning in fourth grade, that amount doubles.[1]

On the rare evening when your child doesn't have homework, you might continue the pattern with a quiet time. During that time, your child might write letters, read, or do other solitary activities. Scheduling a quiet time can help your child gradually ease into, and then maintain, the "homework every night" routine. Respect his work time; avoid scheduling trips to the shoe store and haircuts during this extension of your child's work day.

Help Your Child Prepare a Work Space

Ideally, you and your child should plan and set up a study space together before the school year begins. However, the study space can be established at any time and in many places. Some children find a desk in their bedroom is an ideal place to work.

Whenever possible, let your child make decisions that will affect the shape of his work environment. For example, encourage your child to gather pencils and pens, to choose whether he'll face the window, and to decide if he'd like a clock at his table.

Your child's work area should include:

- good lighting.
- a chair. Even if your child prefers working on the floor, a sofa, or his bed, provide a place where your child can sit upright if he chooses. Your child will always write in cursive now, and he needs a chair and table that allows him to practice the good form he's learned.
- a writing surface. A desk, a table, or even part of a table is fine. Your child will need space to spread out materials since he'll be taking notes from his textbook and occasionally using several references at the same time.
- a secluded place. Your child should not be able to hear or see a television, video game, or radio. If your child says, "I work better with noise," let him add the noise only if he demonstrates the truth of this claim by working up to his potential. Begin with a quiet environment. It is ideal if your child can work in a room with a door he can close.
- supplies. Beginning at about fourth grade, your child will need a dictionary. He might also need an atlas and a calculator. Older tweenagers might need a thesaurus. Add these items to your child's birthday

or Christmas list so he will have them when he needs them. Your child will also need pencils, erasers, pens, scrap paper, a wastebasket, and possibly scissors, a compass, a protractor, and a ruler.

In addition, your child might need supplies that help him become more organized in his approach to studying. He might benefit from a bulletin board. Our daughter Christy writes out assignments each night and posts the list on the bulletin board over her desk. Then she crosses out assignments as they are completed. Every day, she posts a new list. This helps Christy organize her schoolwork.

Your child might use a calendar on which she can record assignments and due dates, a clock, or a card file box in which to store note cards for a research paper. Build costs for materials such as these into your family budget. Investing in supplies and equipment is a tangible way to tell your child, "I support your school work."

If the study space is multifunctional (a kitchen table or a family desk) or your child studies in different homes (with a noncustodial parent or in child care), store supplies in a plastic caddie or box to allow quick, daily setup.

Support Study Skills

An article published by the National Association of School Psychologists makes the following observation: "Being able to study effectively is important for a child's success in school. Many capable students at all grade levels may experience frustration and even failure in school, *not* because they lack ability, but because they do not have adequate study skills."[2] This statement is completely accurate.

Your child will practice study skills in school. During these years, your child will learn how to:
- listen for information.
- read for comprehension or understanding.
- take notes.
- organize and/or outline notes and facts.
- prioritize assignments.

Because the ability to organize is an important part of developing study skills, an increasing number of schools are assuming a more active approach in supporting students in this area. For example, your child might be required to purchase a specific assignment book or student version of a daily planner. A binder with an activity calendar might be issued to each student at registration. Or your child might be invited to a class pizza party or to sign a principal's brag book if he keeps an updated assignment sheet.

When your child is organized, he will have a sense of control over his studies. This sense of "staying on top of things" will be important to your child during these years because he will be required to remember increasingly large amounts of information for tests or apply information to other formats in group projects. These specific elements of learning will happen during typical school days and are often a part of homework.

When your child is organized, he will have a sense of control over his studies.

When your child arrives home from school, he should be able to list assignments, organize his approach, locate and use resources as needed, complete the homework, and prepare his work space for the following day. Practicing good study skills will not happen immediately. Continue to support and encourage your child daily.

Communicate with Your Child's Teacher

During these years, contacting a teacher is generally more difficult than it was in the primary grades. Now your child will have more than one teacher. Teachers can also be harder to locate, since they frequently serve as sponsors for before-school and after-school clubs and activities. Since your child might feel self-conscious about taking a note to a teacher, an alternate approach is to phone the school office and leave a number at which the teacher may contact you.

Your child's teacher needs to know about anything that might impact the school experience. A teacher should regard any information you give him as confidential; however, you might say, "I am speaking with you in confidence and ask that you respect this," just to be certain you have clarified this point. It's a good idea to contact the teacher if you become aware of any of the following situations:

- Homework is consistently too difficult for your child, or there is too much homework on a regular basis.
- Your child never brings home any work.
- Something disturbing happens in your child's life: her dog runs away, her grandfather dies, or her stepbrother moves out.
- You know in advance that your child will be absent.
- Your child is afraid of school or people at school, extremely worried about school situations, or exceptionally discouraged about school, friends, or school-related activities.

- Your child has newly discovered health-related problems: he needs glasses, has a hearing loss, or is on medication that may have side effects.
- Your child does not want to go to school.
- There is a dramatic change in your child's circle of friends, or suddenly he appears to have no friends or is consistently excluded by peers.

You and your child's teacher will attend many school-related events during these years. These casual, social encounters should not become parent-teacher conferences. Avoid the temptation to ask specific questions about your child's progress when you see a teacher at a game, a concert, or an assembly. As a teacher, I have been embarrassed by a parent's stopping me in a crowded hallway to ask, "Is Travis doing better in math?" A teacher can most effectively respond to your concerns when you schedule an appointment and you can both focus on your child in a private setting.

"As a teacher, I have been embarrassed by a parent's stopping me in a crowded hallway to ask, 'Is Travis doing better in math?'"

Participate in Parent–Teacher Conferences

Most schools schedule formal conferences between parents and teachers. Occasionally, conferences will be optional. Participate in every conference regardless of whether your child gets bonus points for your attendance or whether the conference is required. Your involvement demonstrates very clearly to both the teacher and your child that you care about your child and her academic progress.

Conferences are especially important during these years

because, as one teacher explained, "Content in every subject comes along the moment school starts. A child can become lost very quickly." Because of the rapid instructional pace, review your child's progress for every subject area. A child may be doing well in math but not as well in classes that require reading comprehension, for example. In addition, you need to be aware of your child's progress in other areas of development, viewed from the teacher's perspective.

A conference is an information exchange. As a teacher, I prepared by collecting work samples, computing grades, and doing some type of self-evaluation with individual students. As a parent, I prepare for conferences with my children's teachers by writing down questions, comments, and concerns. I take papers or tests about which I had questions. A conference offers an ideal opportunity to clarify facts, correct misinformation, and discuss your child's future.

Arrive promptly and conclude the conference within the assigned time limit. If you need more time, schedule a follow-up session with the teacher.

Let Your Child Practice Problem-Solving Skills

At some point during the tweenage years, your child might have a school-related problem or get involved in an incident that results in disciplinary action at school. In previous years, you quite naturally assumed the role of problem solver. But now, your child will need to take that job.

A veteran teacher said, "Parents don't have enough confidence in kids solving their own problems. One student was having a problem getting organized, but we were working on it and making some progress. It made me crazy when the parent came to the classroom forty-five minutes after school ended. The parent came in dragging the student and rummaged through the kid's desk looking for a textbook. The parent said, 'See. What did I tell you? It was here all the time.' The parent didn't help the student learn anything by doing this."

MIRROR
TALK

The situation that has caused my child the most trouble during this school
*   year is* _____
_____.

When my child gets home from school, the one thing he would probably like
*   to do is* _____
_____.

I know my child's school year is going well when _____
_____.

Your child is probably already learning and practicing some problem-solving techniques under a teacher's guidance. Here's what one sixth grade teacher does:

"I make up a lot of situations so the kids can practice conflict resolution. They need to know that I'm not always going to be around to solve their problems. My goal is to help them learn peer mediation so something doesn't escalate into a trip to the principal's office.

"For example, I'll have the kids act out some situations I make up: 'Somebody cuts in the lunch line in front of you. What can you do besides call the kid names?'

"Or 'You reach for the lunch money in your desk and it's gone. What will you do?'"

As your child gains problem-solving skills, he will need your guidance, too. If your child forgets his history book at school and he needs to prepare for a test the next day, he might need your understanding. If your daughter talks about a classmate who tried to copy her homework, ask questions that will help you form a mental picture of what happened. Then talk about possible ways to respond in such situations.

Remember that in each case, you are hearing about the incident from your child's perspective. As one junior high principal said, "I like parents to know that everything their child tells them may be true—as the child sees it. Parents need to know they are hearing about something through the eyes of a child, and he might not have the whole picture."

> *"I like parents to know that everything their child tells them may be true—as the child sees it."*

As your child deals with conflicts and problems, ask him, "How can I help you?" or "Do you want me to help?" That question conveys your concern but allows your child to determine if he has the skills to solve the problem independently.

Deal Promptly with School Problems

Your child might not be able to handle all situations that come up at school. You will need to become involved if she cannot satisfactorily resolve an issue, if the incident is

11 Ways to Help Your Child Have a Positive School Experience

1. Be a homework helper.

2. Help your child establish a routine.

3. Help your child prepare a work space.

4. Support study skills.

5. Communicate with your child's teacher.

6. Participate in parent-teacher conferences.

7. Let your child practice problem-solving skills.

8. Deal promptly with school problems.

9. Observe the impact of peer expectations.

10. Participate in school activities.

11. Be an informed parent.

repeated, or if it appears the teacher's actions were intentionally planned to embarrass or hurt your child.

For example, one afternoon, one of my children came home from seventh grade in tears. After listening to her story, I was angry at how it appeared she had been treated. I waited at least half an hour to cool down. Then I phoned the teacher and simply asked, "What happened?" I was glad to hear the teacher's perspective of the incident, and I was also grateful I hadn't yelled at her. It had obviously been a difficult situation for everyone. However, my call alerted the teacher that she needed to take action during the next class session and that she could not allow a similar situation to happen again to any child.

Here are some guidelines for dealing with problems at school.

Deal directly with the person involved whenever possible. In a classroom situation, talk with the teacher. If your child was involved in a playground brawl, meet with the playground supervisor. Always begin at the level at which the problem occurred. If necessary, move up the ladder of administration to the principal, the superintendent, or a member of the school board.

Don't prejudge the teacher or the situation. Count to ten, or wait until the next day if you must, but don't draw conclusions too soon and don't try to address the problem while your emotions are high. If your child stomps up to his room and slams the door, find out what happened. If your child's report of the situation seems to require your action or involvement, avoid getting into a "he said-she said" type of conversation with your child or his teacher.

Focus on the problem. Don't go through a laundry list of issues unless each item is directly related to the immediate situation. You have a greater possibility of success if you and school personnel isolate one issue at a time. Set another meeting to resolve other problems.

Be objective. You will naturally want to protect your child. You also want to believe what he has told you is the truth. However, try to adopt an objective position. Say to yourself, "I love my child, but my child isn't perfect. I know he misbehaves at home sometimes. It's possible he misbehaved at school, too." It is not easy to step back from the situation in this way. But what's best for your child is identifying what happened, finding out how your child was involved, solving the problem, and then taking steps to prevent the situation from recurring in the future.

If you respond in an inappropriate way, it will be easy for school personnel to simply dismiss the entire situation as a minor incident blown out of proportion by an emotional parent. Your child will also observe that a tantrum gets action, even though that's not the message you want to send. In the end, the problem won't be resolved.

Take another adult with you to meet with school personnel. If you are upset, it's easy to listen selectively and completely miss things that might be important. Make sure the person understands the role of observer you want him to assume.

Set a time and place for a follow-up before you conclude discussion of a problem. At that time, you can evaluate how well the issue has been resolved and whether or not additional steps need to be taken.

Summarize your meeting in a note. Send the original to the teacher and keep a dated copy for your personal files. Your documentation will be important if the problem is repeated or requires further action.

Observe the Impact of Peer Expectations

Your child will achieve within the social arena of a classroom of peers. This can influence your child's performance in school in various ways. A sixth grade teacher told me:

"Some students are clearly guided by the expectations of their peers. Some want to 'show off' by being a total disruption, or they want to impress others by being the best reader or always getting an A on the spelling test. They do this not for themselves or because it is the right thing but because they want their peers to notice. Students at this age feel forced to do what the expectations of their peers dictate.

"For example, one student walked into the room a few minutes late. Rather than quietly find his seat, he announced to everyone, 'Mr. Barger, I'm late.' Not only was he doing this to get a rise out of me, but he feels the need to be the class clown because that is what his peers expect from him.

"Another student, who has never missed an assignment, always does well, and gets straight As, misplaced the speech he was about to give. Others were not prepared and gave their speeches anyway. But this student knew the class was expecting a great speech from him. He started crying after his two sentence speech. He wasn't upset about how he would be graded but by how the students felt about him after the speech. This is a more subtle type of peer pressure, but it is very real and I see it every day."

One state education official told me quite simply: "The social part of school dominates. The kids aren't there for academics; in these grades, students show up at school for the social aspect."

> *"The kids aren't there for academics; in these grades, students show up at school for the social aspect."*

Peer pressure is a major reason underachievement commonly surfaces during these years. Underachievement can affect a child who functions at any ability level.

Because children don't want to stand out in any way, children on both ends of the classroom performance scale might hide competencies or problems. This is something you and your child have not experienced previously. For example, as a first grader, your child liked to earn stickers for high performance. But now, as a fifth grader, a good performance might make her stand out from the crowd. Earning a spot on the honor roll might not be an honor unless the school has established an environment that affirms and rewards scholarship.

Peer pressure is a major reason under-achievement commonly surfaces during these years.

Because of this desire to fit into the crowd, your child might not want to achieve. Or your child might appear to lack the motivation to do her best.

One educator said, "Underachievement is a complex problem, and it usually takes the student, parent, and school working together to overcome it. Lots of parents in the middle grades feel their kids are underachievers. Low ability and high ability children both want the same thing: to be part of the crowd."

Underachievement can involve many underlying causes; it can also be learned at home or at school. Maintain open communication with your child's teacher so that any problem like this can be identified and discussed immediately.

A desire to fit into the crowd might be observed in other ways. For example, a student who is having problems might memorize answers to use in class without understanding the underlying concepts. Or as one school psychologist noted,

"A child might act out to avoid drawing attention to a lack of understanding class material. Out-of-bounds behaviors might mask feelings of inadequacy. If your child suddenly exhibits problem behaviors at school, arrange to meet with his teacher as soon as possible."

Your child's school day will be shaped by the social forces around him: there is no way you can, or should, change or prevent this shaping. Instead, take every opportunity to learn about your child from these social experiences. Offer to host a school project meeting at your house, to drive students to the area spelling bee, or to take your child's friends home. When you get to know your child's friends, and even schoolmates who aren't his friends, you will have a more complete understanding of his world at school.

Participate in School Activities

Reduced funding for extracurricular activities hits the eight to twelve year old especially hard. In the words of one parent, "Children need lots of opportunities to shine. When they perform in front of people all along as they grow up, they don't know that going onstage is supposed to be scary. They need to hear the applause."

To insure that your child has such experiences, you might need to take an active role or a leadership role in parent-supported activities. You will have greater success in starting or continuing a program if you work with other parents and a faculty sponsor. If a group is already in place, begin by working within that group instead of trying to start another organization. Always try to gain complete support and approval of your school's administrator and board before tackling this kind of project.

The highest rate of parental involvement at school is in the early years. Opportunities for involvement change in nature and decrease in number when your child enters the middle grades. Expect to participate in these ways:

- Phone parents to ask for donations of items or time.
- Serve as a volunteer in the school office, library, hallways, or cafeteria.
- Listen to students read.
- Chaperon students on day trips, overnight trips, or lengthy field trips.
- Identify and contact sources of funding for special projects.
- Support your child in fund-raisers.
- Assist with clubs and activities (organizing and distributing sports uniforms, timing debates, teaching students how to play chess).

Many parent activities may be done in the evening or on weekends. Don't let employment responsibilities limit or prohibit involvement in your child's school. As a PTA president and chair of numerous events in our local elementary and junior high school, I have gained a better understanding of the environment in which my son spends so much time. I've also appreciated the opportunity to observe Matthew interacting with students and staff. My participation has enriched my understanding of Matthew's life in junior high. Perhaps you'll have a similar experience.

Be an Informed Parent

Several years ago your child might have come home from kindergarten with a note pinned to his shirt. The teacher probably felt that was a sure way for you to receive important information.

Now, your child is still your major source of information about school but in a much different way. It might be his responsibility to pick up notices from a table at school, carry home the pages, and then give them to you.

MIRROR
TALK

Communication with my child's school is limited by _____

_____.

The one thing I especially appreciate about my child's school is _____

_____.

I wish I could know more about this aspect of my child's life at school: _____

_____.

If I could change one thing about my child's school, I would _____

_____.

In many instances, the school will help your child be a faithful messenger. One school principal explained, "In our district, on Wednesday, the white envelope goes home. Everything goes home to the parents on that day. If something needs to be signed, that page is run off on paper in the school color. Parents know that sheet is important and they need to look for that. We take seriously our duty to help kids and parents become organized about school."

Your school might prepare information about a field trip, an educational opportunity, or school changes you should know about. Your child might bring it home, but it will be your duty to read and respond. As one mother of three told me, "We talk about every paper from school that comes into this house. We talk about whether it's good or bad. Then there are never any surprises on the report card."

"We talk about every paper from school that comes into this house. We talk about whether it's good or bad. Then there are never any surprises on the report card."

If you have a question, call the school office. Keep track of school events. Post the cafeteria menu, the school play practice schedule, and music contest dates on the refrigerator. You might hear about school issues from a neighbor or car pool driver, but check the facts to be sure you have accurate information.

Wrap-Up

One educator described the way eight to twelve year olds perceive the school experience: "If I'm on the chess team, they'll think I'm a nerd. If I shine in football, that's great. If I shine in academics, they'll make fun of me."

Your child's mental capability is only one aspect of your child's school experience. How he performs at school and how much he enjoys school will depend, in part, on his social skills and how he feels about himself. Because so many factors contribute to school success during these years, you have an important role in supporting, encouraging, and nurturing him as a learner.

During this time period, your child needs to develop and practice good study skills, to learn classroom material, and to do his best on tests and other evaluation tools. This can happen most readily when you and your child's teacher work together. By being involved at school and providing a home environment that encourages academic excellence, you will not only help your child now but set a standard for his future school experiences.

Please note: Even as I write this, major changes might be occurring in your child's school. Several years ago, the Carnegie Council on Adolescent Development published a report titled "Turning Points: Preparing American Youth for the 21st Century." Schools are just beginning to see the impact of this report.

Through the Carnegie Report and the work of other professional groups, educators have identified certain common factors in schools that tend to maximize the strengths of ten to fourteen year olds and most effectively meet their needs. As your child moves into this age range, you might look for a school that offers these features:

- A limit of 200 to 300 students. You can find this size either in a small school or in a "school within a school."
- Specially trained staff members who like to work with adolescents.
- Classes with a thematic approach. Students might work in art, history, science and geography during a study of the rain forest.
- Some emphasis on the social and emotional needs of students.
- Students and teachers working together on teams. Teams might be together for several years.
- Numerous opportunities for students to participate in their school and their community. Service experiences are often built into the school day.
- A pro-parent philosophy. Look for administrators who welcome parent involvement and input; a

formal program for parent observation and participation; availability of resources for parents; school-
sponsored activities for parent networking and
information.

- Assessment that tends to emphasize the positive
  and includes student input. Look for programs
  that ask for parent responses to children's written
  work and that offer various opportunities for
  children to earn grades, including projects,
  speeches, and group experiences, in addition to
  written tests.

Also, be aware that although some recent efforts to be
more responsive to the young adolescent in the school
setting have been encouraging, numerous problems and
challenges are hindering the implementation of more effective educational programs. Be alert for:

- schools that simply change their names (for example, an elementary school that divides into a
  primary school and a middle school) and don't
  change their educational programs to reflect developmental differences of students in various
  stages.
- teachers who are not trained in adolescent development, adolescent counseling, and middle school
  philosophy, curriculum, and instruction; specific
  certification for middle school teachers is still somewhat haphazard and incomplete.
- state mandated and local testing programs or
  course standards that limit local or regional flexibility.

Apply these general suggestions to your situation. There are no perfect schools. However, when you actively seek a school environment designed to meet the special needs of a tweenager, you and your child will emerge as winners.

Chapter 8

Organization and Schedule

As your child moves through the years from eight to twelve, she will have the opportunity to participate in a wide variety of activities. She might attend school and church-sponsored events, be involved with music, join sports teams, and enjoy special interests with accompanying activities. Developmentally, why do most children quite naturally want to participate during these years?

Your child wants to show competence. It's natural that he will want to be involved in as many different kinds of activities as possible. In many instances, he needs practical experience to decide if playing a tuba or tossing the shot put is a good "fit" for him.

Also, your child has become a socially oriented person. This implies that she will want to be around same-age friends. In addition, she will want to do what her peers are doing.

Your child is also motivated to master new skills. He

has an inner drive to achieve and excel. And your child wants to make choices. Selecting her own activities, in a world apart from your family, is one way she shows her ability to make independent decisions.

For these reasons, your eight to twelve year old looks at the world of activities just as a four year old might eye a candy store. Possibilities seem endless. Because you want the best for your child, you encourage involvement, which is good for him or her because there can be significant benefits:

> **Your eight to twelve year old looks at the world of activities just as a four year old might eye a candy store. Possibilities seem endless.**

- Your child can learn to be a team member. She can practice cooperation and discover the elements of fair play.
- Your child can learn about being responsible: keeping a uniform clean, practicing, reaching high performance standards.
- Your child will meet new people and make new friends.
- Your child will learn new skills and practice other skills.
- Your child might discover areas of competence which will influence her vocational direction.
- Your child will achieve recognition and earn accolades.

You might help your child meet a specific goal through an activity. Consider what these parents told me:

"Our kids go to a small school, so we try to expose them

to lots of friends from different neighborhoods. We have a church connection, a swimming pool connection, a soccer team connection. When they are in a single, close-knit group, it's harder on kids socially. Having friends from a variety of backgrounds helps them make judgments about people.

"I've encouraged dance. I thought it was important to take a command in ballet, process it through the brain, and move your body in terms of response to that command."

Such involvement makes this the best of times for some children. These children run, sometimes literally, from one activity to another. They enjoy. They socialize. They shine.

This can be a golden age for parents, too. You know your child's friends. You enjoy being with the parents of your child's friends. Your social calendar is full because of your child's activities.

This can be a golden age for parents, too.

One parent who has supported children in activities ranging from water polo to competitive tennis said, "There's something that every child in the world will be good at. At this age, they have an opportunity to excel. Just find out what your kids' interests are."

But be warned: a hidden danger might lurk against this backdrop of your busy child and supportive family. As one parent noted, "I've got three kids in soccer. I don't know how I'll get through this season." This parent was really concerned. Too much of something, even something wonderful, isn't good. A school psychologist told me, "I see both kids and parents suffering from burnout."

"I've got three kids in soccer. I don't know how I'll get through this season."

Too much of something, even something wonderful, isn't good.

When you and I were growing up, there wasn't so much potential for activity overload. Yet now, as you've seen, this issue affects many families. How did the problem begin?

Activities, Activities, Activities

The large number of leisure-time options available to your child is new to you, me, and others who parent in this generation. Several social trends have contributed to this explosion of organized activities for tweenagers.

- Some families have more discretionary income; more money is available to pay for lessons, leagues, and uniforms.
- The increased number of women in the work force and single-parent families has resulted in children who need something to fill the time from the end of the school day until a parent returns home from work. Children ages eight to twelve are often viewed as too young to stay home alone; supervised group experiences offer a viable alternative for latchkey kids.
- Competition in music and sports is beginning at an earlier age; formal instruction allows children to be more competitive.
- The distinction between childhood and adulthood is becoming somewhat hazy; in some instances, children are being pushed to behave like adults.[1]

The key question for you and me to answer is "How can we find a healthy balance?"

Finding a Healthy Balance

Before your child becomes involved in an activity, find out specifically what the commitment involves. Because there are sometimes hidden aspects of an activity, you might ask:

- Does my child want to be involved?
- Is this activity designed for my child's ability level?
- How will this activity benefit my child?
- How will this activity impact our family life?
- How long does the season last?
- What are the financial requirements (fees, equipment, materials, uniform rental or cleaning)?
- Will there be special performances, contests, recitals, banquets, parties? If so, when is the event scheduled and what is the responsibility of the child and the parent?
- When and where are the practices?
- What are the transportation requirements?
- What is expected of parents?
- Are students expected to participate in fund-raisers? If so, what is each child's responsibility?
- Who is the supervisor or leader and what type of training and experience does the person have?
- Do *I* want my child to be involved more than my child wants to be involved?

Refer to this list when opportunities arise for your child. Before committing to an activity, some parents find it helpful to observe a practice or a performance. Before signing up my children for an activity, I often talk informally with parents whose children are already involved. This type of information gathering helps me determine whether an activity will match our child and our family. You might find a similar technique helpful.

A decision to join or not to join might also reflect family guidelines. One parent explained her family's decision-making process this way: "A musical instrument is a priority because we think of music as an educational, as opposed to a recreational, thing. Everybody must have time for a music lesson in the schedule. Then, we look at sporting activities. I have not allowed them to do gymnastics. With my background as an attorney, it's too scary and stressful for me to watch them do flips on a bar. They just understand that I'm the crazy one on this sport, and they accept it."

Special situations might influence your child's after-school schedule. For example, one family changed schools. The parent said, "To help them get to know kids quickly, the girls become involved in ice skating. That's what many of the kids did at their new school."

You have the right to shape a schedule to fit your child, your family, and your needs.

In another family, sports take priority over church activities. The parent told me, "Brad isn't in the church youth group because he already had team commitments." In our family, we discourage adding activities to the schedule. Instead, we encourage a child to substitute one activity for another. That means Matthew plays only one sport each season; during a school year, he moves from baseball to soccer to basketball. Our family simply could not manage indoor and outdoor soccer at the same time. You have the right to shape a schedule to fit your child, your family, and your needs.

MIRROR
TALK

My child's favorite activity is _____

_____.

The activity in which I most enjoy watching my child is _____

_____.

We prevent activity overload by _____

_____.

The most important reason my child participates in an activity is _____

_____.

As you and your child determine which activities are best for her, reexamine your family priorities. List the pros and cons of joining the science club or taking additional violin lessons. Thoughtfully approach the decision of whether your child should participate in Saturday enrichment classes. Remember that even if one of your children thrived with three after-school activities as a seventh grader, that's not necessarily what's best for every seventh grader: each child is an individual.

Also, your child should understand that an initial commitment to an activity does not imply lifelong involvement. It's all right to be flexible. As one parent said, "The girls do a lot at the beginning of the school year, but they get so bogged down with academics, they do fewer things in spring."

As your child considers options, he might want to keep track of available leisure time for a period of several weeks. This personal time chart can help both you and your child become aware of how he uses his time. Then you can make a decision based on facts ("How much spare time do you have?") instead of making a decision based on perception ("I have plenty of free time").

Once you make a decision together, unless the activity is having a negative impact on your child, help her follow through with the commitment. Your child's coach, leader, or team will be counting on her active participation.

Although making a decision can be challenging, the most difficult challenge might be yet to come. How can you and your child practice problem solving as you juggle a busy schedule?

Practice in Problem Solving

If the calendar becomes overloaded with your child's activities, you will face two major problems: schedule gridlock and coping with stress overload.

One school superintendent said flatly: "With kids this age, individual parents have to take some responsibility. Kids will tend to be over-involved." Taking responsibility means you might need to say no. But because of your child's developmental abilities, she can also help you work through the problem.

Your tweenager is capable of discussing problems. Your child needs to know you trust her growing ability to work toward a solution. Schedule gridlock offers an opportunity to demonstrate how to do this. Encourage your child to use "I" statements during this process. Here's an example:

Examine a situation: "Since volleyball practice started last week, I had to stay up late three nights to finish my homework. On Thursday, I almost missed the school bus because I was so tired when the alarm rang; I turned it off and went back to sleep."

Identify a problem: "I need more time between the end of the school day and bedtime."

Consider possible solutions: "I could drop volleyball (but I really don't want to do that). I could come right home, instead of hanging around the locker room. Or I could go to bed later.

"I could do homework in study hall instead of being a hall monitor. I could eat supper faster. Or I could watch less TV.

"I could use the telephone less (but I really don't want to do that). Or I could do homework faster."

Select a solution: "I'll do my homework faster, and I'll come right home from the bus stop."

Reevaluate after a trial period: "It's sort of working, but I still need more time. I guess I better not watch so much TV."

Encourage your child to use this type of problem-solving technique, and she will benefit by learning that she can control the schedule. A schedule does not need to control a parent or child. Your child will benefit from learning this fact early in life.

She will also see the value of problem solving. Your child can see immediate, concrete results. And she will also learn that she is competent.

In addition, your child will discover that problems aren't always failures. He can learn from problems or mistakes. And he will gain emotional independence. He does not need to depend completely on you to work through situations.

Once you and your child have gone through this problem-solving process, you can prevent or cope more efficiently with any special stress.

Offsetting Stress

There is no magic formula to calculate how much involvement is too much. There is also no way to automatically determine when it's time to completely stop or simply limit the intensity of a specific activity. But it is clear that too much activity can produce stress.

Stress is how your child's mind or body responds to a real or imagined change, challenge, or threat. Some pressure is inevitable. During these years, your child will naturally feel stress before a big test, a dance recital, or a class party. Some of that stress may be good; your child might have a better performance in the school talent show if he's slightly edgy. The challenge is to help your child find the right balance. A little pressure can encourage maximum effort, but too much can cause your child distress.

How do you know if your child's activities are creating unwanted stress?

If your child doesn't have time to occasionally just sit, daydream, write letters or keep a journal, play with neighborhood children, talk to friends on the phone, or even be bored sometimes, then perhaps it's time to reexamine his schedule. Also be alert to these warning signs: he performs poorly in school; he shows signs of irritability; he cries or tires easily; he spends more time alone. Or if the emotional tone in your home seems to be frantic or hassled and family members are continually on edge, take some steps to reduce the pressure.

Sometimes, a schedule problem does not relate directly to your child's activities. During these years, you will probably face two "rush hours" in the weekday schedule: the hour before your child leaves for school in the morning and the hour around supper. If you feel stressed and your child's activities are not the problem, begin a chaos-reduction plan by focusing on one of these two time segments.

Early Morning Hours

To reduce morning problems, encourage your child to make many "morning" decisions on the previous evening. For example, your child can choose his clothing, pack his backpack, and prepare his lunch. Then help your child learn to manage his morning time. Both boys and girls will spend increasing amounts of time in front of a mirror before leaving for school. Build these extra moments into the schedule.

Both boys and girls will spend increasing amounts of time in front of a mirror before leaving for school.

One of our daughters was always running late. When I asked her to write down how she spent her time in the morning, here's what Angela recorded:

Minutes	Activity
10	shower
15	blow dry hair
10	eat breakfast
5	choose what to wear
5	pick earrings; get dressed
5	put on shoes, tuck shirt in pants, make bed
5	put in contact lenses
5	brush teeth
10	do chores
10	brush hair
10	go to bathroom and wash hands

This schedule is typical of a child this age, and it reveals a lot about Angela's development. Just a year ago, my husband and I couldn't pay Angela to run a brush through her hair. But when I asked her why it now takes ten minutes to brush her hair before school she told me, "My hair is an important part of my life." Her appearance has become increasingly important. After looking at Angie's schedule, I told her, "I think Dr. Azar would be delighted to see you are now spending so much time brushing your teeth!"

How did we solve this problem with the morning rush hour? Instead of choosing to pick out earrings or clothing on the previous night, Angie decided to get up fifteen minutes earlier than anyone else in our house. Now that she's a teenager, Angie still gets up early to reduce morning stress and leave the house on time. The schedule she developed as a tweenager continues to work well for her.

MIRROR TALK

To me, stress means _____
_____.

My child might define stress as _____
_____.

The most stressful time of the day is _____
_____.

The most stressful time of the year is _____
_____.

Evening Hours

The evening rush hour can be crammed with frantic activity. I've said on more than one occasion, "I have ten minutes to serve supper between picking up Angie from cheerleading and getting Matthew to school for basketball practice." In addition, because this rush hour comes at the end of a day, all of us tend to be tired and a little edgy. Does your family face a similar problem? If so, consider some of these suggestions:

"I have ten minutes to serve supper between picking up Angie from cheerleading and getting Matthew to school for basketball practice."

- Post the evening schedule on the refrigerator for easy reference. This will prevent you from having to answer repeatedly, "What time is . . . ?"
- Don't answer the phone during dinner. That's what we do during supper. Another family turns on their answering machine.
- Set aside a time for everyone to talk about his day. This can prevent the chaos of everybody talking at once when family members first come home.
- Follow a snack policy. Have a ready-made after-school snack waiting for your child in the refrigerator or on the kitchen table. Regardless of when a tweenager arrives home, she will be hungry.
- Join a car pool. Spend less time as a chauffeur. Car pools will cut down on your time behind the wheel.
- Do only what's necessary during the evening. Prioritize. Don't squeeze more than you have to into these already overloaded hours.

These actions can reduce everyday schedule problems. But you might also want to prevent schedule overload during specific times of the year which can be more stressful.

Specific Times of the Year

Remembering the anniversary of the death of a loved one or pet, getting ready for vacation, or hosting a party for your twelve year old can be stress-filled occasions. Even very positive or happy times can produce unwanted anxiety. Often, stressful days on the calendar follow the same pattern year after year: the summer day when the asphalt driveway is sealed; the autumn day when the sandbox is dumped and the pool is cleaned; Easter or another holiday when the relatives come for dinner.

Some of these days may not be directly stressful for your child; however, because your child is now old enough to be helpful and involved, he might be more aware of the emotionally-charged atmosphere than he was in previous years.

For example, in the days just before leaving for a summer trip, your tweenager might have a seemingly endless amount of energy. Channel that work potential into some extra household chores that your child can now handle. Figure 8.1 is a vacation countdown during the week before a summer vacation for one family with tweenagers.

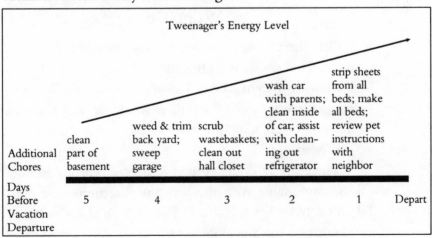

Figure 8.1

This family actually captured tweenage energy and applied it to meaningful projects. Look for similar opportunities in your family just before a birthday party, sleep over, or family reunion. Your child won't respond positively to anything approaching "slave labor" but now has the ability and emotional maturity to contribute in significant ways to the family.

Your child can now work with you toward the common goal of reducing stress by planning ahead. Involve your child in setting and meeting this goal.

For example, a child who is excited about hosting a sleep over can spend time looking through the video guide and compiling a list of movies that might be rented. She can accompany you to the grocery store and select snacks for her friends. She can vacuum the basement rug where the sleeping bags will be spread. Your tweenager's investment in pre-activity work not only provides significant assistance but also reduces schedule overload and offers a chance to practice newly developed abilities.

Wrap-Up

One parent told me quite frankly, "My kids are overloaded. That comes with this age."

Another parent said, "I don't believe you have to structure every hour of a child's day. Have a little down time: don't pack it all in."

Who is right?

There isn't a single correct response. But one mother feels comfortable with the way she determines her children's activity level. She told me, "I look at each activity and what it gives the child. At the beginning of the school year, I work out what can be done in the afternoons after school. We approach this from a family standpoint: Who wants to do what and when can it be scheduled? Sometimes they want to do something, and it just doesn't fit the family."

You and your child must evaluate schedule options within the framework of your family life. Consider the needs and strengths of each child. Look at what's good for all of you. Work through some options. Identify ways to reduce pressure on you and your child.

You and your child must evaluate schedule options within the framework of your family life.

The years from eight to twelve can be full of busyness. When that busyness is a plus, you and your child will benefit from the activities.

Chapter 9

Making the Break:
Parent and Child

I was sitting in the bleachers at a local school gym when I observed a parent struggle with the issue we'll discuss in this chapter.

Our fifth grade boys basketball team was involved in a close game. At halftime, the score was tied six to six. At the end of the third quarter, the score was tied again at ten.

One of our players went up for a shot. Austin made the basket, but took an elbow to the head. Austin's mom, sitting just in front of me, immediately stood up and moved toward her son, who was now sobbing. As the coach went out on the floor, Pam slowly settled back down. She sat with hands clenched, tears in her eyes.

I reached to put my arms on her shoulders. We watched the coach examine Austin, judge the injury to be minor, and send him back to the game.

Our fifth graders lost that game, but Pam took a step forward in giving Austin the emotional space to grow up.

Years ago, you began to help your child build a strong emotional base. When he was very young, he developed a sense of security. He built on that foundation as he learned to control his own behavior. Then, in a flurry of "why" questions, he explored limits and developed a sense of independence. Now, he has been learning new skills and feeling a sense of mastery. If he hasn't already, your child will soon begin to develop a clearer idea of who he is. He will see his own identity apart from yours.

You have probably observed very clear signs that your child has completely left early childhood. Here's what one mom observed:

"I really felt a sense of sadness and loss when it became apparent I had no babies in my house anymore. Learning to read gave Jon a sense of independence. It was one of the major accomplishments that defined him as not needing Mom as much. This happened gradually. He had never been clingy, but we had been compadres. Now, he added his own items to the agenda of the day. It was his becoming a person, a separation from me. With my first child, it was more of a shock. With Jon, I knew this time would come, but I hadn't anticipated this to happen so early."

> *"I really felt a sense of sadness and loss when it became apparent I had no babies in my house anymore."*

This mother was following the words of the familiar saying, "Give your child roots; give your child wings." She was experiencing the same thing I've discovered: the easy part was building the foundation; the challenge is to let go.

A father told me, "You have to start giving them rope, allowing them to develop. This was hard for me. Here's a great student, a great kid who wants to go with friends to the movies. How can I say no? I try to see that they've earned the right to do this, but it's been so hard for me to let them go."

"You have to start giving them rope, allowing them to develop. This was hard for me."

Although the statements from both parents reflect an emotional struggle, the mother and the father quoted above showed signs of effective parenting. They recognized that their children needed more emotional space. They acknowledged that this time is difficult for them. For a child to show what he can do and know who he is, the parent must give permission for this growth to occur.

How to Support Your Child's Independence

You and your child will experience a very real transition during the years from eight to twelve. Here are eleven ways you can support your child during this time:

You and your child will experience a very real transition during the years from eight to twelve.

Give your child the opportunity to learn. As your child learns what he can do, he begins to gain a sense of who he is and who he can become.

A fourth grade teacher explained, "Some parents would prefer to make a child's bed instead of having a child make his own bed. Then, all of a sudden, their child meets the fourth grade teacher who says to the student, 'This is your homework.' The child is overwhelmed. I can easily tell which students make their own beds."

Believe that your child is capable. Your child won't suddenly gain a sense of responsibility and act independently, but she wants to show and practice her new abilities. Give her a chance to do so.

An educator who has taught third, fourth, and sixth grades told me, "It's so important that parents demonstrate how much they trust kids. I've had parents come in and ask me, 'Susie says there's a test on Friday. She says it covers the fourth chapter. Is she right?' When this happens, I try to show that I know how tough it is to trust the child. After all, my own children are twelve and nine. But I point out the positive: that the child has shown she can be responsible to know what's happening in the classroom."

Respect your child's physical space. If something happens on his turf—school, the neighborhood, the car pool—let him handle the situation if he can. Avoid rescuing him. Get involved only if absolutely necessary.

> **"By fifth grade, kids know how the system works. They know Mom can call the principal and get them out of detention."**

A junior-high principal said, "By fifth grade, kids know how the system works. They know the game. They know the rules. They know Mom can call the principal and get them out of detention. If parents call the office and complain, the parents need to be sure they know what they are doing. One of these days, they aren't going to be there to defend their kids."

Accept your child's level of performance. Most parents want their child to jump the highest, throw the fastest, and earn the highest grade. That's normal. But when you want your child to be the best at everything, you are setting her up for failure. In this respect, your child is just like you: she cannot be the best at everything.

When you want your child to be the best at everything, you are setting her up for failure. In this respect, your child is just like you: she cannot be the best at everything.

"A child at this age tends to take responsibility for everything," a school psychologist explained. "So if a child loses a student council election, the child will interpret the loss as a deeper failure if the parent says, 'Oh, you didn't make it. How come?' Instead, the parent needs to say, 'There's more to life than student council.'"

Remember that your child is still a child. The size of her feet might fool you, but she is still a young person. Don't expect more than is developmentally appropriate.

A school principal told me, "What really surprises me is how involved the parents get in this boyfriend and girlfriend business. They give advice about breaking up and talk about how 'she treated him so bad.' This kid is ten years old, and the mom is talking about commitment!"

Make a distinction between what is good for your child and what you wanted to do as a child. Don't use your child to relive your childhood or to fulfill your unrealized childhood dreams.

Don't use your child to relive your childhood or to fulfill your unrealized childhood dreams.

One parent was dealing with this identical issue when we talked. The parent said, "We're at a crossroad with band. Kari hates band with a vengeance. I feel music makes a person well-rounded. We're exploring options. If she drops band, that's her choice. She will have to live with it. Kari didn't ask for any gifts for her birthday: she asked to quit band! I wanted to play an instrument when I was a child. My brother quit drums after my parents bought an expensive set. When it was my turn, they said, 'No. We had a bad experience with your brother.' I want Kari to have what I didn't have, but she doesn't want it."

Accept the person your child is becoming. This step can be one of the most difficult aspects of parenting tweenagers. One mother admitted, "I see how extroverted I am and how extroverted their father is. Our children aren't. I have to watch myself so I don't constantly push them to do things they don't want to do. I was on student council forever, but my fifth grader didn't even want to try for it. I said, 'But you want to do that. Student council members are the leaders in the class.' Allison told me, 'I can do other things.' It was like a light bulb went on in my head. I said, 'Allison, you are exactly right.'"

> **"I was on student council forever, but my fifth grader didn't even want to try for it."**

Continue to support your child as he makes decisions. Your child cannot use adult logic yet, but she is developing mature thinking skills. You will probably face numerous situations during these years that reflect this transitional time in her cognitive development. Be patient with yourself and your child. Know that sometimes you or your child might make a mistake in judgment, but that your child is likely to survive.

Know that sometimes you or your child might make a mistake in judgment, but that your child is likely to survive.

"I've seen how our area has gone from being a small town to having a city atmosphere," one parent said. "The violence in the schools worries me. I worry about Shannon moving to junior high this year. She's going to be exposed to a lot of different kids. When you let them go, you hope they remember a lot of the things you told them. So many of the decisions they make now, they make when they're out of your sight. But they have to learn to make those choices."

"I worry about Shannon moving to junior high this year. When you let them go, you hope they remember a lot of the things you told them."

Help your child interpret decisions. It's quite possible that neither you nor your child will understand every situation that affects him during these years. Not everything that happens to him will be rational or fair. Your child will need an adult perspective to help him deal with these almost-inevitable incidents.

One parent said, "We decided our eight year old would not play soccer this year because she was assigned to another first-year team, and she had played first-year soccer last year. Jenny said, 'I don't think they wanted me because I didn't score a goal.' We found out it was a clerical error by the league office, but Jenny took it personally. She needed help to understand that the mistake wasn't a reflection of her ability."

Encourage independence whenever possible. Preadolescents

typically experiment with clothing, hair styles, and other accessories. Whenever possible, accept your child's choices so she can practice living with her decisions. This approach also allows you to provide specific input, direction, and rules in areas of greater importance.

Whenever possible, accept your child's choices so she can practice living with her decisions.

As one mother said, "Sometimes we fight over clothes that aren't appropriate. I want Courtney to look like a young girl, not a streetwalker. She likes to roll her shorts too short. We've had disagreements over that. Usually, my husband reminds me, 'That's not worth fighting over.' I have to remember to let Courtney have some autonomy. I have to remind myself that these little things are just differences of opinion."

Find the proper balance between helping your child and going overboard with support. There's a fine line between being involved and being overbearing. Use these four guidelines to help you determine the right balance:

- Develop a fulfilled life apart from your child. Do what makes you a happy, healthy, productive human being.
- Respond to signals from your child that say, "Back off." For example, your child might say, "Mom, I don't want you to drive me to soccer. I can get there myself."
- Don't internalize your child's ups and downs. Don't get too upset if he gets a low score on that math test or science project. He earned the grade; he will learn to live with the consequences.

- Support your child by talking, listening, praying, chauffeuring, and being available. Now that she's growing up, you will not always need to be physically with her to be supportive. One school psychologist advised, "Stay in touch but don't hover."

Trusting Your Child to Be Completely Independent

The two final challenges of independence relate directly to issues of self-care: allowing your child to stay home alone and allowing him to baby-sit younger siblings. Self-care relates directly to your personal development as a parent and your child's development as a preadolescent. Your child's readiness for new responsibilities, a sense of independence, and a desire to show mastery all come together at this time.

As is true in many parenting situations, self-care begins slowly and builds gradually. The first time you leave your child alone in the house might be on a Saturday morning when you run next door to deliver a hot meal to a sick neighbor. Your child will know exactly where you are, and he might even be able to see you through a window.

Selecting the right time to begin self-care is not simply a question of age. Use your knowledge of your child, your child's input, the nature of your neighborhood, the availability of a trusted neighbor, and the checklist below to influence your decision. Most of all, trust your gut-level feelings to determine when your child is ready to be home alone.

Before you leave your child alone while you walk the dog around the block or run to the local gas station, you will need to prepare her with basic information. Your child should know all of the following:

Exactly where you are going and how long you intend to be gone. Always overestimate the amount of time you will be gone so that your child will not worry if you are not back when you expected.

Whether he should answer the phone. If you want your child to answer the phone, give her a script of what to say and keep that note by the phone. For example, tell her, "If Grandma calls, you can go ahead and talk and tell her I'll be right back. If anyone else calls, say, 'My dad can't come to the phone right now. May I take your name and number so he can call you right back?'"

How to respond in an emergency. Act out what to do if the smoke detector goes off, if the guinea pig gets loose, or if the dog won't stop barking. Many parents choose to enroll tweenagers in a baby-sitting class. This is an excellent way to ensure that your child receives safety information and training. Whether or not your child is actually going to baby-sit, a valuable part of the course is usually "What to do in an emergency." Contact your school, local hospital, or community organizations to find baby-sitting classes.[1]

What to do if the doorbell rings. Review the procedures you want him to follow for answering the door. In general, most families decide to leave the door unanswered if a child is home alone. If you make this choice, be very specific about whether you want your child to peek through the curtains or look through a peephole to see who is there.

Before beginning any form of self-care, discuss with your child the advantages and disadvantages. Don't give up your place with a baby-sitter or an after-school child care provider until you are certain a permanent change will be successful.

At whatever age your child starts his self-care, begin by using the guidelines listed above. Some eight or nine year olds might feel perfectly comfortable to be left alone for a short time (five to ten minutes) during the day. A six year old might be fine when left "alone" for a brief time with a nine-year-old sibling. But a ten year old generally should not be expected to care for several younger siblings. Remember, too, that the time line for your child may be different from that of other children the same age. Carefully plan your child's experiences so that your child's and your own "home alone" comfort zone will expand at an easy pace.

Continue to work toward leaving your child alone for longer periods of time or after dark. Move carefully toward daily self-care before and after school. Maintain your previous daytime child care arrangements until your child is completely ready for this major step. Locking a door, carrying a key to school, and coming home to an empty house all require a maturity level far beyond staying at home for a few minutes while you shop for groceries.

Locking a door, carrying a key to school, and coming home to an empty house all require a maturity level far beyond staying at home for a few minutes while you shop for groceries.

"I know of kids who experience added stress all day at school because they are worried about going home alone," said a school psychologist. "I encourage parents to check with the child's teacher to see how the child is functioning at school after self-care begins."

MIRROR
TALK

When I think about leaving my child at home, alone, I _____
_____.

One concern I have is _____
_____.

One thing that would be helpful is _____
_____.

I wish _____
_____.

Bye-Bye Baby-Sitter

At some point during the tweenage years, your child will leave the baby-sitter era. I knew our family had reached this point when our oldest child was almost as old as the baby-sitter and one of the children told me, "We can stay alone." I was delighted at the prospect of not having to drive twenty minutes in a driving snowstorm to take a sitter home, but leaving a child in self-care can be one of the most difficult aspects of parenting a preteen.

In another family, it was time to move to self-care when the sixth grader started to balk at "being left with the little kids in the YMCA after-school child care," recalled the parent. "Carmen had a friend who lived near us, so we talked with her parents. We decided to let the girls come to one of our houses, after school one night a week. We didn't know how this was going to work. We explained the house rules to both girls, and we communicated frequently to be sure the situation was mutually beneficial."

Here is another parent's experience:

"Last year, my daughter said, 'I know more than the

baby-sitter.' Moving away from using a sitter was not at all hard for the children (ages nine and twelve). But it was a hard step for me to take.

"Moving away from using a sitter was not at all hard for the children. But it was a hard step for me to take. You sit there and imagine everything that could go wrong."

"We gave Mindy a key and let the two of them catch the school bus at the corner in the morning. After school, they came home alone and let themselves in. We set up rules like, 'You may not leave the house until Daddy comes home,' and everything worked out well.

"It was really hard for me the first few times. You sit there and imagine everything that could go wrong. You call a hundred times. Then gradually you think, 'They can do it.' Now they won't have a baby-sitter at all, unless we're going to be out very, very late.

"I was guided in all this by other parents. A lot of Mindy's friends were being allowed to do this also, so this gave me a guideline that said, 'It's OK for a twelve year old to have this responsibility from time to time.'

"This has been a big freedom for me at this stage: I don't have to dial the phone for an hour, looking for a baby-sitter just so I can go out and shop for a birthday present.

"This year, Jake will be alone for fifteen minutes after school every day before Mindy gets home from junior high. He'll walk home with another ten year old who is in the same situation.

"This has been a real learning experience for me, a real letting go for me. I've been pleased with the results."

If your child is ready to be home alone after school, develop written guidelines with and for your child. In addition to the basic "home alone" points noted earlier, consider these factors that can affect the success of regular self-care.

Arrival: Act out with your child, the procedure to follow if your child arrives home and finds a broken window, an open door, or anything else out of the ordinary. Your goal is not to scare your child but to heighten his security awareness and give him confidence that he can handle various situations.

Check-in: At least initially, have your child phone you or another adult immediately after arriving home. You might schedule your afternoon coffee break at the office around the time you expect your child to phone. Then you can take time to hear about the school day when your child is most eager to talk.

Emergency numbers: Keep phone numbers and a pencil and paper by the phone. Since pencils might tend to disappear now that your child is into the heavy homework years, tie a pencil to the phone.

Routine: Your child should have a basic, even if brief, list of what to do upon arrival at home. Your child can gain a sense of security and competence by following a routine. The list might look like this:

- Call Grandma
- Open the back door for Skippy; wait at the door while he runs around; let Skippy back inside and lock the door
- Give Skippy fresh water
- Open mail addressed to you
- Eat a snack if you wish

- Practice flute
- Follow directions for starting supper
- Begin homework

Snacks: Specify what kind of food is acceptable, how much can be eaten, and which appliances can be used.

Phone use: Whether or not your child comes home to an empty house, your eight to twelve year old might still enjoy talking. The phone is often a preteen's link with her whole world. Work with your child to develop guidelines for appropriate after-school phone use.

Siblings: Siblings can help or hinder satisfactory self-care. This depends on the age of the children, the number of children, the relationship between siblings, and individual personalities. If you have more than one child who will be in self-care, work through completely and reevaluate regularly how your arrangement is working. Your children will need to know how to resolve disagreements without your presence, influence, or involvement.

Friends: Friends should not be allowed in the house or yard. Although some parents allow their child to leave the house to visit friends, self-care is most successful when the child stays home.

Extras: Encourage your child to enjoy this new freedom. He might want to turn on the radio (louder than what you're comfortable with) or listen to music you don't enjoy. In your guidelines, include specific information on whether your child can watch television, play video games, use the computer, or play in the backyard. Also, give your child choices in the schedule whenever possible.

Wrap-Up

"There is a time for the parent to move on. This is that time," one school psychologist told me.

The educator who said that knows about the struggles for parents in the gap: she is the mother of three and grandmother of five. Unfortunately, I've found her words are easier to say than to do. For me, staying in the protective mode was very comfortable. After all, that's how my children and I have grown up. We've been together. Now it's time for us to leave the nest.

I have moved slowly and carefully. I have stopped along the way to think. At times, I have hesitated.

I have moved slowly and carefully. I have stopped along the way to think. At times, I have hesitated. Perhaps you will do the same. I can encourage you, though, to take the steps necessary to make the break. There is a wonderful relationship and great joy ahead: you will begin to enjoy the new person your child is becoming.

Chapter 10

A New Look at Old Issues

Some issues crop up repeatedly during the seasons of parenting. If you sometimes feel, "I've been here before with my child," you're exactly right. As parents we cross the same turf again and again. How you handle an issue changes as your child's level of development changes. The solutions that work for a younger child probably do not apply now. Some of these issues come from the everyday fabric of our culture. Others, like death, are universal human issues faced by every parent in every culture.

If you sometimes feel, "I've been here before with my child," you're exactly right. As parents we cross the same turf again and again. How you handle an issue changes as your child's level of development changes.

Here's an example from our society: When your child was three years old, you limited the number of TV cartoons your child watched. The issue of appropriate viewing habits resurfaces when your eleven year old asks to watch an adult-rated movie.

Or you might have taken your preschooler to library story hour to encourage reading. Now, you might wonder just how to get your nine year old to start reading again.

Years ago, your son accepted the dime you gave him for clipping coupons every week; now, he wants to know why you won't give him a twenty-dollar advance on his allowance.

But everyday problems are not the only issues we face again and again as our children grow. Death, which is a natural part of the life cycle, is also a topic which will reappear. You might have sensitively handled questions about death when your father was very ill six years ago; now that another murder was reported on a local news program, your ten year old seems to have more questions about death.

You will probably talk with your child at least once about television, reading, money, and death during the years from eight to twelve. Let's examine each of these issues as they affect your parenting a preadolescent child.

Television

Many parents have a love-hate relationship with the TV: television is a great baby-sitter when you need to cook supper in the ten minutes between the saxophone lesson and soccer practice; it's the great invader when your son wants to leave Grandma's birthday party so he can get home to watch a favorite show.

What is the role of television in your family? Gather some information. Find out how much time family members invest in viewing. Simply put a paper and pencil by the

TV. Ask every family member to record the "on" and "off" time every time they watch TV for a week. Add up the number of hours. Then discuss television viewing with your tweenager.

Television plays a role in the life of many preteens. On the playground, an eleven year old can join the "in crowd" during a discussion of the latest made-for-TV movie. Through the magic of television, a nine year old can travel to a world far away from the classroom, where today she was the first one eliminated from the spelling bee. A twelve year old who made an error in the ninth inning of a Little League game will enthusiastically identify with his favorite major league team in the World Series.

Obviously, TV offers some payoffs for preadolescents. But you might observe some of the drawbacks right in your own living room. One parent with an eight year old expressed concerns about television content. After being a single parent for more than three years, this person told me, "I don't want my daughter to think a typical family is like a family on TV." Perhaps your eight year old drops swear words into a conversation; after questioning him, you discover those words are used on a television show he watches after school at the baby-sitter's house. I notice that after watching a couple of hours of football, my twelve year old has pent-up energy that gets directed, usually in a negative way, toward the nearest sister or cat.

Television impacts parenting more dramatically now than in any previous generation. As one parent confided, "The most critical issue in our family is the kids' free time. TV is a hot topic. It's probably the biggest issue right now. I am appalled and amazed at what my kids are exposed to. When they were younger, I put an hourly limit on TV. As they get older, it's harder to do that."

> *"The most critical issue in our family is the kids' free time. TV is a hot topic."*

As this parent indicated, by the time a child reaches the age of eight or nine, many families become concerned about the role of television. Unfortunately, viewing patterns are generally already in place by this time in your child's life.

MIRROR
TALK

I really like television when _____
_____.

I dislike television when _____
_____.

If I removed the television, our family would _____
_____.

My greatest concern about TV is _____
_____.

If you want to reduce the importance of TV in your family, you will need to make a conscious effort to change viewing habits. Gaining complete control of television will require some changes on your part. For example, when you are trying to fix supper, and your child asks, "Can I watch TV until we eat?" it is easy to say quickly, "Yes, yes, go ahead." It's harder to say, "No. Write a letter to your grandparents or read one of those books we checked out from the library yesterday." You will need to take the time to list for the baby-sitter what TV programs your child may watch. And when you tell your child to turn off the TV, you will need to help him find something or someone to fill up that empty time.

When you tell your child to turn off the TV, you will need to help him find something or someone to fill up that empty time.

Encourage your child's creative suggestions and ideas. Consider rewarding his wholehearted participation in solving the television dilemma, perhaps with dinner at a restaurant or a visit to a local museum.

To take control of TV:

Consider the ways your household facilitates television viewing. Ask yourself:

- Is the living room furniture arranged for viewing the TV?
- Does my child have increased viewing options with cable television?
- Is the television always available?

If you answered yes to these questions, you might want to limit TV access. For example, you might choose not to subscribe to cable television. You might choose to have only one TV. Ask your child to help you rearrange furniture so that conversation, not viewing, is encouraged by the room design. You might purchase a cabinet in which the doors can be closed in front of the TV when it is not in use.

What ideas can your child contribute? Ask him.

Help your child discover other leisure time options. As a preteen, your child has many activity alternatives. As one parent observed, "When kids are making good grades and involved in activities, there won't be time for TV. The key is to get them outside to play and get them involved." Or you might establish a trade-off plan to insure a variety of leisure time options. For example: one hour of television is matched with one hour of reading or playing games; or, the family signs up for roller skating lessons at a local rink using money previously designated for cable subscription services.

Make conscious decisions about program content. Your tweenager can help choose appropriate programs. In our home, each Sunday afternoon, my husband and son sit down with the television listings and a marking pen. They work together through the weekly listings and highlight programs that my son may watch. If you are uncertain about a program, you might videotape the show for your personal preview to determine suitability for your child.

Or, since your child has developed more mature thinking skills, you might develop a family list of viewing criteria. Simply review with your child a list of what constitutes objectionable content. For example, if a show contains inappropriate language or sexual innuendos or situations, agree together that the program will be turned off permanently. Use this opportunity to show your child how you make value judgments. Your child will develop a sense of what is acceptable.

Don't depend entirely on published guidelines and standardized ratings to guide your viewing decisions. You know best what is right for your child at this time in his life.

Be aware of television habits. Is your child a channel flipper? Is she a couch potato, complete with potato chips? Develop guidelines that will support your chosen approach to television and decide what foods, if any, will be allowed in the viewing area.

Determine a family policy toward advertising and program previews. Some commercials can be offensive even if the shows they interrupt are not. You might turn the TV to "mute" during commercial breaks.

Shape TV time to fit your family. One mother of three

said, "Way back in the 1950s, I had a mother who limited television. My husband and I talked about the idea of completely removing the television from the house. We decided, instead, to set rules. There is no television during the school week. Saturday morning they may watch; then they may choose one weekend night to watch. That's it."

Or you might use a token system to control the amount of viewing time. There are a variety of models for this technique, but basically, once a week you give your child a number of chips, index cards, play money, or coins. Each token can be cashed in for a half hour of television. When the tokens are gone, the TV stays off until the next week.

Variations of this basic program might include the possibility of earning extra tokens by doing extra chores; allowing siblings to trade or sell tokens; trading tokens for items purchased at a bookstore; or selling tokens back to parents. Any type of reverse "pay-per-view" route can be risky, however: one mother told her sons that she'd give them a dollar for every day they didn't watch any TV. In less than four months, each boy had earned a hundred dollars!

Be firm about your guidelines. If you decide to watch television until nine o'clock, turn off the TV at nine o'clock. Stop your child before he uses the remote control to "cruise" other programs.

Consider the TV-free option. "TV is such a time consuming drug," one parent said. If you feel that the negatives outweigh the positives, you might choose to totally or almost completely eliminate television in your home.

Act thoughtfully and carefully if you choose this option. Try going TV-free for a week or a month before you make a final decision. Involve all family members. Listen carefully to your tweenager. Consider having a small television, available for use with school assignments or to view special broadcasts or important news reports.

There is no question, that living in a no-TV home will impact your preteen. As one parent admitted, "The kids complain. I do feel a pang of guilt when people say, 'Didn't you let your child see that wonderful program?' But I also know there are wonderful outside games to be enjoyed, computer programs to be played, and books to be read."

You must decide the role television will continue to play in your family life. It's clear you can tame the tube; and you can, if you wish, selectively choose programming that has the potential to enrich your child's life.

Television, and other high tech forms of home entertainment will become more appealing to your child in the next years. Interactive devices, large screens for home use, virtual reality, and additional audio and video components will combine to create technology even the most creative ten year old can hardly imagine. The decisions you make now will influence your child's life during these years and will affect the way he approaches his leisure time options in his future.

Next, we'll discuss reading, an alternative activity that directly competes with television and high tech entertainment for your child's leisure time.

Reading

Your child has learned to read. He can now read the nutritional statement on the back of the cereal box, write a letter to Grandpa and address the envelope, and read the directions aloud as you attempt to put together his new bike.

But parents of tweenagers typically complain, "My

child doesn't read as much as he used to." It might appear that way, but consider the whole picture. Your child is probably:

- reading for information and comprehension at school.
- reading in various formats: the box score in the newspaper, comic books, or the statistics on the back of a baseball card.
- reading directions to a video game on the screen.
- writing letters to relatives and pen pals.

Reading is a self-contained activity. But you still have an important role: you can encourage reading; you can be alert to typical preteen preferences; and you can take various courses of action if your child doesn't want to read.

The decisions you make now will affect the way he approaches leisure time options in the future.

"Have your child read to you so you can assess how he is doing," suggested the parent of a fourth grader. "You might be surprised. You might even say, like I did, 'Wow, I thought he could read better than that.'"

MIRROR
TALK

Using a single word, I would describe my child's feelings about reading as ___
_____.

The last time I saw my child reading was _____
_____.

I think my child's favorite book right now is _____
_____.

(Ask him to verify your perception.)
One book I hope my child will enjoy is _____
_____.

I share my feelings about reading when I _____
_____.

How to Encourage Your Child to Read

Generally, a child in the age bracket of eight to twelve years old does not have the amount of time available for recreational reading as in previous years. However, you can continue to support his reading with some of the same techniques you used when your child was younger:

Keep books handy. Can your child take ten steps from his bed or favorite chair, and find something appropriate to read? Easy availability of reading materials is still important.

Model reading. You are reading this book: that's good! As the parent of a ten year old advised, "Set an example. If a child needs to do more reading, let him see you read. If it's important to you, it will become important to the kid."

Read with your child. In earlier years, you might have shared a bedtime story. Continue this pattern even if you only read together a couple of times each week. Set aside time in advance, though. Reading a single chapter will take much longer than reading several picture books. Also, you and your child might want to discuss what you've read.

Give books. Post your child's wish list on the refrigerator, and ask your child to continually update the book list. You will then have a convenient way to make suggestions to relatives and friends who are shopping for Christmas or your child's birthday. A book is a gift your child will open again and again.

Encourage letter writing. Many children in this age range enjoy having a pen pal. Often, fourth and fifth grade teachers set up a mail exchange with a class in another geographic region. You can do this at home, too. Your child might get the name of a missionary child from church or write regularly to a cousin or the child of one of your distant friends. Your child will read mail that's addressed to him.

Have a regular "family read." This is one tradition that can easily grow up with your child. Begin by looking for an activity you do together regularly (eat a leisurely Sunday breakfast, go out to dinner on Friday) and simply add reading time to what's already on the schedule. Or set aside a specific time, perhaps ten minutes after supper, when everyone in the house reads. Your tweenager might read a sports card price guide, and you might read the newspaper, but the whole family reads.

Some Preteen Preferences

Your preteen has probably developed some strong preferences about the types of books or specific authors he prefers.

Your child might reread the same book. One dad told me he didn't believe his daughter when she said, "I've read this book twenty times." But she had. The girl had even memorized parts of the dialogue. Your child might do something like this, too.

With all the changes swirling around your child during these years, he might seek something comforting and familiar. A favorite book can be even better than a friend during this time. Preadolescent friends are fickle; a book can be counted on. So don't be surprised if your child wants to check out a certain title from the library yet another time. That particular book is obviously meeting a need.

A favorite book can be even better than a friend during this time. Preadolescent friends are fickle; a book can be counted on.

Your child might have only brief time periods for recreational reading. Short articles often match the available time frame better than books. Magazines are ideal (see Appendix B for magazines targeted to preteens).

Your preteen might be very selective. It's not unusual for an eight to twelve year old to read only a certain type of book. Your child might read through an entire series of books about one character or written by a particular author. Often, your child's choice of reading materials will be strongly influenced by media, advertisements, and peers. At a school book fair, for example, one series might sell out completely to fourth graders; but that's fine, because fifth graders wouldn't think of reading the same titles.

Your child might find inappropriate reading material. Just because your child is reading at this age, it doesn't mean that reading is good for him. Horror, violence, inappropriate language, and sexual situations find their way into some preteen titles. Generally, however, your child should make his own reading choices. Tread carefully before imposing censorship. If your child has chosen material that you feel is questionable, read it along with him and then discuss your concerns.

Buy your child good books; then he will have a standard by which to judge others. There is good reading material available for your child that doesn't focus on fear, capitalize on goose bumps, or tantalize with sex.

Watching you look through a book section will help your child develop sound selection techniques. Encourage your child to look beyond the cover of the book; covers are designed to sell books. Covers on preadolescent titles can be especially misleading. Show your child how to skim through an early chapter or read the table of contents to get an idea what a book is really like.

Use school book lists for ideas of appropriate authors or titles. Trade lists with friends and relatives whose children attend different schools. Your child might only want to use such lists as a guide, however, as some titles might be inappropriate. (See Appendix C for recreational reading suggestions.)

If Your Child Doesn't Want to Read

It's possible that your child might be "turned off" to reading. Some tweenagers don't enjoy books. If that's the case with your child, don't push. Simply keep printed materials available. If you are concerned, however, that your child might have problems with reading skills, consult her teacher: Don't delay. But if the problem is simply lack of interest, these suggestions might also be helpful:

Provide reading related to a special area of interest. Your child might read a sports biography, a foldout book on castles, or the story on which a favorite movie or video was based.

Consider your child's current interests and find a gift book that relates to one of them. At this time, relationships are important, especially to girls. Your daughter might enjoy books with an element of innocent romance; your son might like a book on soldiers who fought together or a baseball team.

By observing the books your child is reading, you will see without prying what's important to him.

Find a book that comes with something else. For example, a book titled *Teach Yourself Tap Dancing* might come with a videotape, or *Make Money with a Lemonade Stand* might include an advertising banner.

Also ask your child's friends for the titles of books they've read recently. The best recommendation for a book might come from another ten or twelve year old.

Provide opportunities for your child to apply what he reads. Remember, during these years your child is looking for meaning and relevance in what he learns. For example, you might ask your child to compare the ads for two grocery stores to determine where you'll do the weekly shopping. Or, as your child is putting together a model, you might casually comment on how reading and understanding the directions contributes to the successful building of a model.

Weed your child's books. Your child's reading level and interest areas have changed dramatically in just a couple of years. You and your child can go through his collection to make room for new (and thicker) books appropriate to his age. He might even discover reading materials he didn't know he had.

Your child might enjoy trading titles with friends or selecting books for a neighborhood garage sale. A garage sale might even earn something that preteens love: money.

Money

Money isn't new to your eight to twelve year old. The typical preteen enters these years with three basic money-related characteristics: he likes money, he knows how to spend money, and he would always like more money. Does your child fit that profile?

The typical preteen enters these years with three basic money-related characteristics: he likes money, he knows how to spend money, and he would always like more money.

Your child is already functioning in the world of finance. An eight year old who wants a new pack of baseball cards might ask, "Do you have some work I can do for money?" A socially aware or spiritually sensitive ten year old might dutifully put some allowance money in the church offering.

But your child will still have a limited understanding of the value of money. I remember when my daughter Angela was about eight or nine. She was eager to go to the bank. She wanted to deposit all the money she had received for her birthday. She had a huge amount—thirty dollars—which Angie thought would pay for a year of college!

Your eight or nine year old will be able to understand what it means to save money for a specific, short-term goal. For example, if your child wants to earn ten dollars for a new football, you might set up a "matching payment" type of plan. He can earn $1 a week doing extra chores, and for each dollar he earns, you will contribute a dollar to the football fund. Because your child is still very concrete in his thinking and is concerned about fairness, put your agreed-upon dollar in the money jar at the same time he does each week. At the end of five weeks, your child will be able to buy the football.

Your preteen is looking for ways to declare independence. Money can become a flashy, if not a completely correct way, to show that freedom. An eleven year old might spend birthday money from her grandmother on a face cream which a friend said helped her pimples. After looking at the ingredients listed on the label, you conclude the expensive miracle cream is basically hand lotion in a fancy jar. Or perhaps a twelve year old will want to purchase a name brand watch with money he got for Christmas—not because he likes the watch but because he wants to show off to friends.

During these years, you will be his primary teacher and financial advisor. Consider the following list of six statements your child should be able to make by age twelve:

"I can identify money by feeling it and by looking at it." Your parents actually had an easier time teaching this concept than you will. In these days of plastic money, it's harder to help a child learn about coins and bills.

First, identify what your child knows about money. Ask your child to reach into your purse or pocket and pull out a quarter or a dime—without looking. As she grows up, your child will need to be able to identify a coin by feeling when it's dark and she's at a phone booth or later, when she's driving and needs toll money.

For paper money, play a guessing game to help your child learn how to visually discriminate between denominations. He can use this skill the next time he's in a hurry and needs to check the change received. Ask: "Whose picture is on a dollar bill? A five? A ten?"

"I know what these words mean and I can use them correctly:

checking account, charge, interest, credit, tithe, budget, salary, bargain, offering, taxes, change, balance."

Use proper vocabulary when you discuss financial matters. As you use the words, define them. Then see if your child can use the same words properly as your conversation continues.

"I can't spend more money than I have." Tell your child about deficit spending, but don't let him practice it. This means you should not allow an "advance" on his allowance or on gift money that he expects to get for his birthday.

"I can earn money." Encourage financial enterprise. An eight year old can run a lemonade stand during your garage sale. You will need to help your child plan her venture. Make sure she thinks about supplies like lemonade, ice cubes, cups, a table, a chair, a pitcher, a money box, change. Help her decide how much to charge.

An older child might consider various locations for the stand, make several signs, or brainstorm other ways to make money at the same time, perhaps adding brownies or some other treat to their enterprise.

Your eight to twelve year old can use research skills at the library to find books and resources that suggest age-appropriate jobs. Our tweenagers joined with neighbors to sell advertising to support a neighborhood newspaper. Your child might start a house or pet sitting service for the summer, or baby-sit, or do odd jobs for neighbors. Encourage your child's creativity, then help and support his efforts.

"I can manage the money God gives me." A well-known millionaire reportedly said that he taught his daughter how to manage money with three boxes. Each time she received money, she was to put one-third in a box to spend, one-third in a box to save, and the final third in a box to give away.[1] If your child used this popular multiple bank

concept when he was younger, he can now continue the idea in the same way or adapt it to paper transactions.

Some parents help their older children open a checking account and then pay them for jobs by writing a check. This procedure has two immediate benefits: children gain experience in recording checks, banking, and balancing a checkbook, and they establish the habit of not cashing the entire check for immediate spending.

"I can make wise purchases." Preteens are influenced by peers and tempted by advertising targeted to young people. Knowing that your child is surrounded by incentives to be an impulse buyer, model how you go about making a thoughtful purchasing decision. For example, if you are buying a new stove, let him go with you to comparison shop. Let him track the various features of the different brands. Get his input before you make a decision. Let him practice the thinking process associated with wise buying.

MIRROR
TALK

As a child, I learned about finances by _____

_____.

One thing I want my child to understand about money is _____

_____.

For my child, money _____

_____.

Your child will learn many of these concepts by your direct teaching. She will also learn about money by listening to what you do and what you don't do with your money. Your child will be confused if you teach him to give a certain percentage of his money to the church or a charity and then he sees you slip a single dollar bill into the offering plate on Sunday morning.

Teaching your child about money matters does not imply that your child has the right to know the balance of your bank account. As I previously noted, a preteen does not have a realistic concept of value. However, you will find many opportunities to actively involve your child in discussions and activities concerning money without compromising financial confidences.

As you consider the learning opportunities you are providing for your preteen in this area, you'll need to answer the question, "Should my child get an allowance?"

Allowance

During the preadolescent years, you and your child will probably have at least one discussion about allowances. An allowance offers your child hands-on experience with money management. Parents usually give an allowance from one of two basic perspectives. Either the child earns an allowance by completing specific chores in a satisfactory manner; or the child receives an allowance as his part of the family income, and it is not based on chores, grades, or behavior.

Here's how one mother described the allowance experience with her two children (Brett, age nine; Stacey, age twelve):

"When the kids were little, my husband and I started an allowance system. We started because my kids got into a 'want, want, want' syndrome. I was tentative about allowances. We started with a basic amount and then increased the kids' responsibilities through the years. They have certain responsibilities they must achieve by the end of the week to get their allowance.

"If they want something extra, they have to get it from their allowance. When we stay at a hotel with an arcade, if they want to play a game, it comes out of their allowance. And they still have to kind of approve their purchases with me.

"With Stacey, I will put money toward tennis shoes up to the cost of a pair that I would normally buy for her. Then if she wants a name brand, she'll need to add the extra amount. She would rather have one name brand pair of shorts than two no-name pairs, but the procedure is the same: I set aside a certain amount of money and she decides. We will pay for Stacey to get into the teen center on junior-high nights, but if she wants snacks when she's there, she buys her own.

"Brett could be the world's biggest spender if he didn't have some limits, so his allowance has helped him. When that old ice cream truck comes through the neighborhood, Brett might say, 'I'm saving money for some new arrows, so I won't get ice cream today.'

"I think my kids understand more about money than I did when I was this age. Brett is very interested in why one child has a certain jacket and he doesn't. He and Stacey are aware of the money situation around them because there's so much clothing and accessories available for their age group.

"I can look back at allowances over a five or six year period, and the allowance system has worked well."

"Allowances? What a mess. The whole thing fell apart in a month."

Another mother told me, "Allowances? What a mess.

"My husband was going to pay the kids every week to do stuff. The whole thing fell apart in a month. Now, they're back begging me for things because they don't have spending money."

These two families had completely different experiences with the allowance system.

An allowance can be a useful technique when the reason for it is clearly understood, the agreed upon amount is paid on schedule, and both parent and child understand what the child is expected to buy from the allowance. In some families with tweenagers, an allowance is increased because the child is expected to purchase a school lunch, school supplies, or some clothing. Begin an allowance system only if you intend to invest your time and effort to make the program work.

Begin an allowance system only if you intend to invest your time and effort to make the program work.

Saving, spending, and other money matters have challenged you, your parents, and grandparents. But in the next section, we'll discuss something far deeper and more serious. As your preteen experiences more of the real world, he will come to a new understanding of the finality of death.

Death

During the years from eight to twelve, your child will face death in at least one of two ways: through news reports of a tragedy or natural disaster or through personal experience with someone he knows. No matter how your child encounters it, death is never an easy topic. Even the word sounds ominous and threatening.

My father was a pastor, so I quite naturally attended several funerals as a child. I remember my dad leaving the house, even in the middle of the night, because someone was dying. But the concept still seemed rather remote until I was twelve years old and my mother was diagnosed with cancer. That was the first time death came so near I could almost touch it.

I was twelve years old and my mother was diagnosed with cancer. That was the first time death came so near I could almost touch it.

Whether or not death will affect your immediate family, death is more than a word to your preteen. Your child now has the mental capability to understand that death is final. He knows that people who get cancer or who are in a coma sometimes die. He hears news reports and realizes that death sometimes comes to children his own age and to parents like you. Because he distinguishes between fact and fiction, he recognizes the difference between the violence he sees on a video screen and Grandmother lying in the hospital hooked up to a breathing machine. He can also accept the fact that Jesus Christ died for his sins and offers him eternal life.

How to Talk about Death, Dying, and Serious Illness

Talking with your child about issues of life and death that affect him personally is seldom easy. You may be tempted to avoid such discussions because you don't know what to say. Here are some guidelines that should help you.

Be honest. Explain the facts as you know them. If you don't explain truthfully, your child might imagine something far worse than what actually happened. Here's how one parent explained to a ten year old that his grandfather had died:

"Jonah was very close to my dad. It was a school holiday when Dad died. We had been with him in intensive care that morning. We had just gotten back home when the call came. I sat on the couch. Jonah and I held each other. I told him what the doctor had told me: Grandpa had a reaction to the drugs."

Your child's response to the situation might be similar to your response. If you can cope honestly, your child will be encouraged that he can cope, too. One mother, who had been diagnosed with cancer three weeks before we talked, told me how she and her husband shared the news with their children:

"We did a lot of the talking. Our children aren't the kind who will run to their rooms and cry. We tried to explain everything about the cancer to them. We had a positive attitude. We felt informed. We were honest and didn't hold anything back."

Encourage your child to express his emotions. Your child needs to talk about what she is feeling. She might be angry, sad, upset, or afraid. She might feel a sense of loss or of abandonment. Your child might say very little at the time. It may take him a while to put feelings into words. These are normal reactions. I talked with one mother two weeks after the death of her ex-husband, who was the father of her eight-year-old daughter. Here's what this mother shared with me:

"I told her that Daddy probably would not be coming home but that we would keep him in our prayers. We had told his relatives that we wanted Grace to say good-bye to her daddy when the end was near. He was only sick for two weeks, and we got a phone call that the time had come.

"I was so resentful. I had to tell my little girl her daddy was dying and it was time to go and say good-bye. I wanted to go in with her. It was so hard sitting in the waiting room, and my eight year old was alone, telling her daddy good-bye. They took Grace out before they removed the machines, and then they took her in again to see him after he had died.

"I was so resentful. I had to tell my little girl her daddy was dying and it was time to go and say good-bye."

"Grace didn't grieve. She didn't show anything. We were waiting for some big explosion. It never happened. Now, two weeks later, it still hasn't happened."

Your child will have his own timetable for grief. He may talk about the death long after you or other family members have experienced a sense of emotional closure. There is no standard length of time for the grieving process. Here's how Jonah, a ten year old, coped with a death:

"He would talk about it a lot at night for a whole year. 'Do you think Grandpa can hear us? What's heaven like? Do you think Grandpa can see us?' I don't think Jonah ever blamed God for Grandpa's death, but he asked, 'Why did God want Grandpa?'

"Now he doesn't talk about the death so much but just makes comments like, 'Grandpa would have liked to see me at this game.' Jonah got out his pocketknife the other day and said, 'This is the knife Grandpa got me.' It's been two and a half years, and he still remembers. I put a snapshot of him with his two grandpas, one of whom is still living, in his bedroom."

Realize that your child's grief is separate from yours. When a relative or friend dies, acknowledge that your child had a personal relationship with that person that was different from your relationship. Jonah's parent said, "One thing that helped him was that a friend sent a flower arrangement to him, personally. It was just strictly from a friend to a friend. It was a basket of ivy with a bird and bird's nest on the top. Someone recognized that Jonah had a loss too."

Take the opportunity to talk about eternal life. One mother, who worked through the death of her husband with her daughter, said, "I don't know how people who aren't Christian could ever explain death to a child."

The girl was almost nine years old when her father died. She, like your child, could accept, with some understanding, the promise Jesus makes: "I am the resurrection and the life. He who believes in Me, though he may die, he shall live" (John 11:25 NKJV). Your child, like this preteen, can now understand the purpose of prayer and offer prayers from the heart for those who are critically ill and for those who mourn. When your child deals with death at this age, she will have a more mature understanding of life with Jesus than was possible just a few years earlier.

As a twelve year old coping with the very real possibility that my mother could die soon, I was caught up in new tasks of everyday life: doing the laundry and learning how to cook more than meat loaf and baked potatoes. Even though my daily focus became preparing eatable food, I remember that my mother often talked about heaven as being a place where she would have everything she needed. I often imagined her corner of heaven would be full of the African violets she loved. That simple picture I drew in my mind, with Jesus next to my mom in her heavenly garden, gave me a certain sense of peace when I was twelve years old.

MIRROR
TALK

As a child, I remember one person's death affected me. It was when _____
_____ .

One concern I have about talking to my child about death is _____
_____ .

My child talked to me about death most recently when _____
_____ .

My child believes this about eternal life: _____
_____ .

How to Talk about a Tragedy or Disaster

The concepts outlined above can also apply when dealing with a tragedy or disaster that does not impact your child in a personal way. But be aware of some additional factors.

Your child might want to take some action. Let your child be a part of relief efforts. A tweenager might not be as overwhelmed when he can participate in helping those who survive. Allow him to collect canned goods from the kitchen shelf to donate to relief efforts or mail a card to a friend.

Two children might respond differently to the same event. After hearing the same news program, one child might have nightmares; another won't appear to be affected in any way. A parent of an eight year old and a twelve year old observed, "A recent area murder triggered many questions from my younger girl. She wanted to know everything: 'Where was the murder? How did it happen?' She wanted specifics. My twelve year old never asked anything."

Your child wants to know what is happening, but he might

need help to interpret and understand. For example, a news broadcaster might refer to "Santa Ana winds" or "hurricane-force gales." Ask your child if he knows what those terms mean. Explain where those phenomena of nature occur or help him find more information.

Two days after a large earthquake, I talked with the father of two girls whose home was located near the epicenter. He said, "Since the quake, we've had major aftershocks. I'm nervous, and I know my nervousness has showed as we've cleaned up all the glass. But we've talked, and I even drew a picture of what causes the aftershocks. We've talked about why they occur and how we can react." With the girls' increased mental capability, they were able to understand some facts about earthquakes. A sensitive dad helped them interpret what was happening.

Your eleven or twelve year old will be able to understand longer-term effects of a tragedy. For example, after an oil spill along a coast line, your child might ask, "What happened to the birds and fish?" Be ready to answer his questions about the implications of any disaster.

A tragedy close to home may remind your child that he could experience a similar situation. One parent noticed the effect on an eight year old: "We live near the place where a murder recently occurred. Now, my boy is worried that a 'bad man' is going to come into our house and get him."

"We live near the place where a murder recently occurred. Now, my boy is worried that a 'bad man' is going to come into our house and get him."

If your child feels this way, begin by acknowledging that the event happened. Your child is old enough to read the newspaper account of the disaster, so follow up by discussing any specific questions or concerns he has. Then assure your child that it is normal to be afraid. When possible, be calm and reassuring. Walk around the house with your child and point out the locks on the door. Test the smoke detectors. Review the script you've taught your child for dealing with an emergency.

Wrap-Up

These four issues—television, reading, money, and death—will come up repeatedly as you parent your preteen. Occasionally you and your child might have intense feelings and become almost consumed with settling an issue related to these topics. When you find yourself getting off on a tangent, reread some of the guidelines highlighted in this chapter.

The ebb and flow of parenting is seen so clearly when you take a step back from the four issues highlighted here. Reading will be a primary focus when your child is eight or nine years old. This will be true especially if your child faces any kind of academic problem. By the time your child reaches seventh grade, reading will decrease in importance as a parent-child topic. Taming television can be an explosive family issue throughout these years. Once your child becomes a teenager, TV will decline as a focal point.

During these years, you will lay the groundwork for the lifelong challenge to understand both money and death. These issues may generate a highly emotional response from both you and your preteen. Your child's patterns and attitudes about money matters will be shaped during this time. Of course, death is a totally different topic. Because death is a natural part of the life cycle, there isn't a single age at which every child learns a set number of new facts about death. Experiences, not age, trigger teachable moments. During these years, you will share a perspective of death, dying, and eternal life with your child who is gradually developing more abstract thinking skills.

How and what you discuss with your preteen about television, reading, money, and death will depend, in part, on your ability to communicate. This important topic is the focus of the next chapter.

Chapter 11

Communication

Communication has been important in your parent-child relationship since the first time you held your newborn baby. Now you are experienced at reading your child's written, verbal, and nonverbal messages. But be prepared: what, where, and how you and your child communicate will change dramatically as he moves through the preteen years.

Here's how one mother observed this change approaching with her eight-and-a-half-year-old daughter:

"I feel she's starting to build up walls. I see this most of all when we talk. She doesn't elaborate with her answers. When I ask the same question I did six months ago, I get a shorter answer now.

"I'll say, 'Oh, you look so pretty in that outfit.'

"Before, she would give me a cuddle and ooze in the mommy warmth.

"Now, she is matter-of-fact and says in a very offhand way, 'I know.'"

In our family, I've had a simple request to pick up his shoes turn into a lengthy disagreement with my twelve year old. Dinner table discussions about what happened that day sometimes end with Matthew picking an argument with his sister. In your family, you might notice that the child who once told you everything now answers questions with a casual wave of the hand.

You might notice that the child who once told you everything now answers questions with a casual wave of the hand.

Because the pattern of communication changes so dramatically during preadolescence, it's easy to fall into the trap of crisis communication—talking with your child only when there is a major problem or when you are upset. Crisis communication is a part of life, but it will be less necessary and less traumatic when you talk to your child throughout the day. Continue to discuss, laugh, share joys and sorrows, write notes, and answer questions during everyday happenings. Here's one parent's example:

"We were stopped at a red light. An orange pickup truck with a bunch of boys pulled alongside. Sam [Samantha] looks older than some of her friends and has matured already, and the boys started catcalling. Samantha had a perplexed look on her face.

"'Mom, those boys are whistling at me.'

"My daughter complained, 'Mom, those boys are whistling at me.' I just said, 'Boys will do that sometimes. Just ignore that when it happens.'"

"I just said, 'Boys will do that sometimes. Just ignore that when it happens.'

"The light changed and we moved on. I was frightened.

Sam was surprised. I was glad, though, that we could talk about what happened."

Askable Parents

The mother who shared this story is an *askable parent.* When her daughter didn't understand what was happening in a simple, everyday situation, she asked her mother to interpret the incident. The mom did this. She also suggested an appropriate response. This is the type of healthy communication you will want to continue with your child during these years.

It's possible that your child might hide true feelings from you. Personal privacy is important; sometimes that carries over to sharing feelings. Your child might be worried that you'll yell if he tells you, "I failed the math test." Or your daughter might feel embarrassed to tell you about the seventh grade boy who tries to touch her in inappropriate ways. Sharing what's in her heart might not be easy for your child to do—or for you to hear.

MIRROR
TALK

Within the last week, the best talk I've had with my child was about _____
_____.

I know I understand what my child is telling me when _____
_____.

When I don't understand the point my child is trying to make, I _____
_____.

I show my child that I'm paying attention by _____
_____.

It might not be enough to say, "I'm here. Talk to me." Although your child has learned many ways to communicate, she still might have difficulty putting feelings into words. She might not know how to tell you what she wants you to hear. If this is a problem, encourage your child to write a note. Follow up in a conversation later. Also let your child know you understand it's sometimes difficult to talk.

In addition, encourage your preteen to pray regularly. She needs to know that God will always listen and respond. Model effective communication, and when appropriate, share your emotions with your child. These are all good ways to prioritize communication.

Stay continually alert for communication opportunities. As one fourth grade teacher advised, "If your child wants to discuss something, work with that. Don't just say, 'I'm busy, now.' If your child wants help with math, help him. So often, parents put help on hold. That works against your child. Work with your children, not against them."

Tips for Communicating with Your Preteen

Your child will generally say at least something if you are approachable. That means you take seriously what he says, listen attentively, respond when your child initiates conversation, and invest time and effort in communication. These are characteristics of an askable parent. Also consider these additional points:

Nonverbal communication speaks as loudly as words. If you want your child to be honest, don't grimace when he says with an ominous tone, "Can I talk to you?" As one mother said, "I tell my daughters [ages eight and nine]: I am your best friend. If you've broken the law, if you're pregnant, come to me. Mom and Dad will help you deal with it. You can always come to me. Don't ever be afraid to tell us something, no matter how bad it is.

"When Carson [age eleven] climbed into the car one day, I knew something had happened.

"He said, 'I got a detention.'

> **"When Carson climbed into the car one day, I knew something had happened. He said, 'I got a detention.'"**

"I said, 'I appreciate you telling me. I'm glad I didn't hear it from the principal. Tell me about it.'

"Carson knew I would be disappointed, but I was glad he told me."

This mom might have gripped the steering wheel a bit tighter, but her overall, nonverbal response to her child must have conveyed, "I'm listening. Tell me." Otherwise, her son might have just said, "Aw, forget it," and ended the conversation before it even began. The parent's nonverbal communication supported the openness of her words. Because of the way she responded, her son will probably be willing to talk with her again about a problem.

Also use your child's nonverbal signals to help you understand his mood and general outlook. Your child's actions often give very clear signals. It takes time and practice to learn how to read these changing messages.

> **Use your child's nonverbal signals to help you understand his mood and general outlook.**

Teach as you talk. The way you live tells your child what you value in life. But during daily, normal conversations, you can underline what you believe. You might talk about the use of alcohol as you and your son walk by the liquor section of the grocery store. You can support your child when she tells you about the shoplifting a friend considered. Perhaps you could affirm the importance of good time management when your child studies geography notes while letting her fingernail polish dry.

In just these three simple examples from everyday life, a child could learn about family values, the parent could practice being an askable parent, and the child could receive positive reinforcement. These kinds of opportunities happen many, many times during a single day! When you use these everyday opportunities, your child will respond by sharing in the same type of conversational tone. In the following situation, notice how easily this tweenager gives her mother some fairly significant information:

"We let our daughter go to the junior-high dance. When she came home, the first thing she said was, 'People were kissing. I thought it was pretty disgusting. They were kissing right where people could see it.'

"We let our daughter go to the junior-high dance. When she came home, the first thing she said was, 'People were kissing. I thought it was pretty disgusting. They were kissing right where people could see it.'"

"I asked, 'What did you do?'"

"She said, 'I told the teacher who was in charge.'"

"I said, 'I'm glad you felt that way and I'm glad you told the teacher.'"

Attending the dance gave this eleven year old the opportunity to test her personal values in a social situation. When the parent stayed askable and didn't fall apart and say something like, "You saw kids kissing. Why that's terrible!" the conversation continued in a very positive way. The child left herself open for parent feedback. This parent not only responded but also helped her daughter work through feelings and perceptions. This parent caught a teachable moment and used it beautifully.

Respect your child's confidence. Your child needs to be able to trust you, just as you want to trust her. One mother discovered this the hard way. She was willing to share her story:

"I made a blunderous error as a parent. When my daughter was in fifth grade, I allowed her to go to a party. Nothing serious happened, but in casual conversation I shared with other parents what my daughter had told me about a relatively minor incident of kissing and hand holding between two of the other students. I made the error of aligning myself with the other mothers instead of with my daughter. I allowed myself to betray her. I should never have done this.

"I could not have foreseen what would happen as a result of this. The repercussions of this giggly little party incident were magnified in these kids' minds and their social group. It caused my child a lot of grief and a lost friendship. To this day, the child who was involved in that harmless situation and got in trouble for it hasn't forgiven either my daughter or me.

"I went through a terrible period, about two years, to regain my daughter's confidence. Now, she knows I will keep anything she tells me confidential. You couldn't torture information from me. I don't share anything that isn't public information. You can't allow yourself to be aligned with other parents if doing so betrays your child in any way.

"My advice: if your child is that wonderful child who does confide in you, treasure that. Never, never allow yourself to betray that relationship. Know the information, use it in the way you deal with your child, but keep it to yourself."

Practice good listening. By definition, communication involves giving and receiving information. Listening to your child and encouraging her to listen will continue to happen as a part of your normal family activities. A parent with a nine year old and a twelve year old said, "We have a lot of family meetings. The kids groan and say, 'Oh, no, not again,' but we believe in family decision-making. And we feel dinner time is a sacred time. When we eat together, we don't take phone calls."

This type of group gathering not only implies to children, "You are important to this family," but also indicates, "I will take the time to listen and discuss." In-depth listening requires total attention. That kind of listening happens most easily when there are few or no distractions.

A meeting format works well for this particular family. But during these years, you will notice that your child wants increasing amounts of privacy for important discussions. In addition, the issues with which your child is dealing are so much more complex than in the past that you might find a need for more individual time. As one parent said, "I always thought you should have family-type activities. But I've found it's better to talk with kids on their own. They are more willing to verbalize feelings if there isn't a brother or sister around. My kids never talk about feelings or give an opinion when we are all together."

Plan to have time alone with your child. Identify several activities that allow you to focus on your child. What works for your friend and her preteen might not work for you.

Respect individual differences. You already see many ways in which your child tells you, "I am an individual." Respect her uniqueness in the area of communication just as you accept her specialness in other aspects of life. This means you won't be able to repeat exactly the same speech on shoplifting, makeup, or manners to each of your children. Every child will probably have a different pattern of receiving and giving information. As one mother told me, "When talking about sexuality, both my kids were different. Kathleen was always a very private person. It was hard for her to talk about this with me. When I brought up the issue, it was always information-based without emotional sharing. She's just very closed about some parts of her life. It's been hard for me to learn to respect that. Naturally, I want to be a part of everything.

"Chris, now eight years old, is much the opposite. His questions are not necessarily questions but rather remarks about discoveries he's made and he wants to inform me."

How your child communicates and what she chooses to communicate will be shaped by the person your child is becoming. Observe carefully how he talks and listens so that you will be able to communicate more effectively.

Although many of the points above contribute to clear communication at any time in a child's life, stay alert for characteristics unique to this age. For example, during one period of time, I felt that one of our children spent more time talking to her friends on the phone than talking to me. After an exciting event, she would race past her father and me to phone a friend. Peer relationships are increasingly important to children at this age. A significant amount of time and effort will be targeted to communicating with friends.

Continue the good communication techniques you

used when your child was younger. For example, in earlier years, you knelt beside your child or bent down to make eye contact. Now that your child is growing taller, you might be able to look at her more directly or sit down across from her at a table. Eye contact is still important.

It may be that all of a sudden your child can talk more openly with his grandparent than with you. Support this cross-generational sharing. Some older people have the patience and share a perspective that even impatient pre-adolescents will respect. As one parent recalls, "When I was about ten or twelve, I remember getting a lot of wisdom from my grandparents. I used to go fishing with my grand-mother. I remember lots of conversations we had."

Factors Affecting Preadolescent Communication

Don't underestimate the importance of your role in communication. Your child will continue to benefit from your input and your active listening. Here's an example:

"For several days after our eight year old's birthday party, I could tell something had happened at the party that bothered her. She would say things like, 'How could people be mean to others?' and, 'I don't know who my best friend is anymore.'

"After a few days, she finally told me what bothered her. Some of the kids had said, 'I can't believe you invited Seth and Nikki to this party.' That bothered her because these children are her friends. She couldn't understand why some of her friends were being mean to others. She had such a sense of fairness that she couldn't resolve this in her own mind. She needed to talk to an adult who would listen."

The child finally discussed the incident because this mom stayed askable. The parent didn't pump for information. She practiced patience by waiting until the child was ready to talk. This patience is especially important to a preteen child who is trying to sort things out in her own mind and establish independence by working through issues by herself. You will see how your child thinks things through during negotiations.

Arguments and Negotiation

Communication will be an area in which your child will practice these new thinking skills. Because he can see shades of gray between two extremes, he might question traditions and routines that he previously accepted. You might get into this type of discussion:

Parent: "Please dust the fireplace."

Twelve year old: "It doesn't look dirty."

Parent: "David, you know the mantel always gets dusted as part of house cleaning on Saturday."

Twelve year old: "Yes, but it's really not dirty. See?"

Parent: "Do it because I say to do it."

Twelve year old: "Why?"

Here's one possible conclusion to this conversation: the parent gets mad, the child stomps off, and the fireplace stays dusty. This scenario is a typical example of a preteen practicing the skill of argument. It's important for you to stop talking when a conversation stalls. Continue talking only as long as the conversation moves forward.

In the preceding example, the parent might have said, "If we wait another whole week before dusting the mantel, it's going to be filthy. That's unacceptable. Dusting is one of the chores you've agreed to do. Please wipe it clean, using a dust rag, sometime before noon today."

When your child practices negotiation, you might become frustrated, but persevere. Your child needs to learn this skill. Dealing with a child who lies, which can be another aspect of communication at this age, can also require patience.

Honesty

You will continue to teach your child honesty through-out the tweenage years. Your child might have tried lying when she was a preschooler. Now, she might try it again. At both times—around the age of three and in preadoles-cence—hiding the truth might be a way to establish iden-tity. During both age spans, your child is also trying out new thinking skills, but now your child can usually distin-guish fact from fantasy.

In preadolescence, hiding the truth might be a way to establish identity.

In addition, by this time your child might have over-heard adults telling social lies such as "I won't be able to join you for dinner because we have other plans" when she knows there are no other plans. Honesty—the lack of which includes being less than completely truthful—must con-tinue to be part of your parent-child communication. As a school psychologist told me, "The home needs to get truthfulness in place. Don't be overly suspicious, but know that by this time, some children have learned not to be truthful because they don't want to face the consequences of their action." By embellishing the truth, other preado-lescents can gain attention or admiration from peers.

One of your goals for communication during this time should be to help your child be honest. In a questionable situation, guide your child to tell the truth by asking specific questions. For example, if a window breaks while your child and his friends are playing outside, don't run out and ask, "What happened?" Instead, ask a series of questions that don't leave much room for imagination:

- Do you know what caused that window to break?
- Did a ball go through it?
- Who were all the people playing with the ball?
- What were you doing when you heard the glass break?

If more than one child was involved, ask the same questions, individually, of each child. Get the facts about a situation, then discuss what happened. Use all the communication skills you have—listening attentively, avoiding blame, talking about the importance of trust, focusing on problem-solving, expressing your sincere care and concern—to help your child practice honesty as the best policy.[1]

Mood Swings

Communication will be directly affected by your child's preadolescent moods. When you are aware of this fact, you will be able to cope more effectively during the inevitable ups and downs.

One parent told me, "I had a wonderful counselor tell me to let my child have a bad day occasionally. I need to allow her that same freedom of expression that I have but not allow her to be disrespectful. That's a tough balance for me every once in a while."

This is good advice to remember on days when conversations with your child seem to end with a slammed door. Every day won't be a good day for both you and your child. At those times, don't force communication. Also, don't assume that isolated behaviors like yelling or breaking into tears on those few days are a sign of a major communication breakdown between you and your child. Sometimes you don't want to talk either!

Occasionally, a child will feel like talking later. If one of our children is mad at me, he or she will sometimes talk with a brother or sister. And sometimes, just a change of location will be all that's needed to change a mood and trigger conversation.

Location

Seize the moment. If your child is available and emotionally open, talk. If your child wants to talk, listen. Grab every chance to communicate with your child. This might mean you snatch five minutes in the car between the orthodontist's office and school or talk while you shop for shoes, but it's important to continue to talk. One parent told me:

If your child wants to talk, listen. Grab every chance to communicate with your child.

"My husband and I spend a lot of time talking about things we remember about our childhoods. We do that on family vacations during those hours and hours of driving. We talk about things that were hard for us or embarrassing. It not only makes it easier to relate to where our children are, but the kids see us in a different light other than just as a perfect parent."

Whenever possible, respect your child's increased need

for private conversations with you. Even if you are discussing a baseball score or a front page news story, your child is very aware of others who might hear or see you talking together. As one parent of a nine-year-old boy observed, "He still cuddles and kisses me goodnight. But now, I can't do that in front of his friends when I leave him in the morning. Now, I just tell him how proud of him I am."

> *"He still cuddles and kisses me goodnight. But now, I can't do that in front of his friends when I leave him in the morning."*

Keep in perspective your desire to communicate. Delay communication until the setting is appropriate for two-way sharing. For example, this means you will avoid talking about a report card on the sidewalk in front of the junior high or discussing your child's overdue haircut while you're driving a car full of soccer players. Even topics that are public information can be potentially embarrassing to a preadolescent. One mother told me of a time she let her good intentions to communicate get ahead of her good sense:

"I wanted to have open communication about sexuality, so I took a class on how to talk to your child about sex. I think you need a support group of people who are going through similar problems to give you the confidence you need to talk about those issues with your children. So often we lack confidence, and so we don't bring up the subject.

"In this class, we got into the topic of masturbation. I realized I had never talked to my eleven year old about that. When I came home, my husband and son were in the bathroom, talking. My husband likes to relax in the tub. I just walked in and asked my son, 'We've never talked about masturbation. Do you have any questions?' My husband sank under the soap bubbles.

"I thought that it was good I felt comfortable talking about this. My husband said later that there might have been a more appropriate time."

The Quiet Child

Some preteens take a quiet approach to communication during these years. Some physically do get quieter: their need for privacy is reflected in a reduced amount of talking. Others don't get any quieter, but the conversation balance shifts from talking with parents to talking with friends. Other children become selectively quieter; their desire to establish identity results in single word answers to questions like, "How was school today?"

If you are frustrated by your child's minimal responses, approach him with the following suggestions in mind.

Be sensitive to timing. Your twelve year old might want to dash to the phone or the refrigerator immediately after school. She might not want to talk about what happened in math class or at volleyball practice.

Write a note. Most children in this age group will at least read a note. Taking the time to write lets her know communication lines are open on your end. Leaving a personal message for her on your answering machine might accomplish the same thing.

Uncover your child's interests. Offer to drive your child and his friends to a school game or take them to the mall. Read a book together. Tune into your child's favorite radio station to learn about the music that appeals to him.

Ask questions selectively. You might be curious, but don't pry. Ask only one question at a time and give plenty of time for a response.

Wrap-Up

Your child's development will be reflected in the way she communicates with you. Watching your child's growth during these years isn't always easy. It can even be hard on the ears! One parent described communication during these years like this:

"The 'I hate you' phase lasted about a year.

"The 'shut up' phase lasted about six months.

"Now, he's ten. The sassy mouth is our biggest problem. He also uses slang. I tell Jason he can use slang with friends, but not around me or other adults. I had to explain what these words meant and why they were inappropriate.

> *"The 'I hate you' phase lasted about a year. The 'shut up' phase lasted about six months. Now, he's ten. The sassy mouth is our biggest problem."*

"I've heard other parents tell their children, 'Don't say that.' I just try and explain why it's wrong."

For all the adult arguments he gives and the four-syllable words your child says but doesn't understand, your child is still a child. During these years, talking with you about real events, situations, and people is exactly the type of experience from which he can benefit. When he has concrete experiences and you are available to listen and interpret them for him, your child learns in a way that maximizes growth potential at this time.

Continuing communication will take additional effort during these years. If you always wait for your child to start talking, you might seldom really talk with each other. You will often need to take the lead. As one mother told me:

"I've found that my oldest son asked me questions related

to sex that he wouldn't even ask his father. Now that he's sixteen, he doesn't ask questions anymore. You have to lay the groundwork and lay it early; later is too late. Whenever there's an article about AIDS that I feel is noteworthy, I share it with my ten and twelve year olds. I've done that so much that now they say, 'Oh Mom.' I believe you have to talk now, while your children are open to listening."

As you communicate during these years, your patience might be tested, your values challenged, and your decisions questioned. You might say some things you regret, ask for forgiveness regularly, and apologize more than you ever anticipated. But in spite of the mistakes, keep talking. Continue to listen. I recommend you follow this dad's advice: "Let your kids know you love them. Adults are so afraid to say that to kids at this age. Parents have to tell kids they love them and that they are willing to support them. That just doesn't happen enough, especially with boys and fathers. Develop a trust and bond. Then say the words, 'I love you and will support you.'"

You might say some things you regret, ask for forgiveness regularly, and apologize more than you ever anticipated. But in spite of the mistakes, keep talking.

If you follow the suggestions in this chapter, you will have a head start with the subject of the next chapter, discipline. Good communication with preteens prevents so many problems. It's a very effective non-discipline technique.

Chapter 12

Discipline and Child Management

This chapter is one of the shortest chapters in the whole book. Is that surprising?

At the very end of the preceding chapter, I hinted at the close connection between communication and discipline. Effective communication can prevent many child management problems.

But consider for a moment how many of the other topics we've discussed also relate to discipline: If you've supported your child's development of good study habits, you won't have a late-night yelling contest that begins, "Why didn't you do your math before you watched television?" If you've helped your child find a healthy balance of after-school activities, your child won't argue about starting guitar lessons and an eight-week session of ice skating during the same month. If you've adapted your parenting to reflect the developmental changes of your preteen, you have mastered many techniques directly related to effective preadolescent management.

Because you already know how to avoid many of the situations which can trigger preteen–parent conflict, we'll now focus on a limited number of concepts: setting appropriate limits, helping your child work through a behavior-related problem, and guiding her to accept the consequences.

Your Child Needs Limits

Your child needs to act appropriately within limits. He also needs to learn to accept consequences of his behavior. Respecting limits can cause problems because some preteens try a casual approach to following rules. For example, your twelve year old might feel that choosing what to wear to a school dance is far more important than choosing to follow rules relating to his choices after the dance. Or your child might feel rules are for younger kids, and she might test parental limits to state her independence. Or your preteen might ignore rules for the same reasons that he was disobedient when he was younger: he might be tired, afraid, hungry, or getting sick, or he might never have been told that a certain behavior was wrong.

Your child needs to understand that he is not exempt from living within the laws of the family and society. This basic fact can be very difficult for some tweenagers to accept. Here's what happened to one eleven year old:

Your child needs to understand that he is not exempt from living within the laws of the family and society.

"We had told Kirstin she could go to the basketball game, even though it was on a school night. She was to call us when the game was over and we'd come and pick her up. We didn't get a call. My husband went out looking for her. She didn't get home until after ten o'clock! One of the other moms had driven a bunch of kids to a pizza place, and Kirstin had gone with them.

"My husband went out looking for her. She didn't get home until after ten o'clock! One of the other moms had driven a bunch of kids to a pizza place, and Kirstin had gone with them."

"When Kirstin got home, she couldn't believe she was in such bad trouble. We didn't allow her to talk on the phone for a week, and she couldn't go to the next basketball game. I know we came down kind of hard, but she needed to see she couldn't just go off on her own like that."

This example is typical of a conflict that results from a preteen challenging her parents' limits. Prepare to face this type of situation: Your child might test rules in a similar way. Refer to these four guidelines as you set limits:

Identify what's acceptable to you. One of the most common complaints of preadolescents is, "But Megan [or Nicholas or Kendra or any other peer] can do it." Define the limits for your own child. You can get input from other parents, but you must decide what is acceptable for you and your child.

For example, one mother was being pressured by her eight- and nine-year-old daughters who wanted to get their ears pierced. This mom told me: "I think my daughters are way too young to take care of pierced ears. The problem is that most of their friends have pierced ears. Their friends are kids we approve of, and we know their parents and like them, but I have to tell my girls, 'These are our rules. I don't care what so-and-so is doing.' The girls may pout. I guess we are a lot stricter with our children than most of our friends."

Clarify rules. Make it easy for your child to behave.

For example, one father tells his children, "I say, 'Be home at 8:23,' instead of just saying 8:30. That's easily understood. Because it's a little different, it helps them remember."

If your child likes to see things in writing, post a rule or chart on the refrigerator. If your child says, "But Dad, I'll forget," suggest he write a note to himself and put it on the mirror (preadolescents spend increasing amounts of time in front of it). State and clarify rules using whatever form works for your child.

Make joint decisions. Whenever possible, let your child be involved in shaping guidelines.

Many preteens live under a basic house rule: everybody helps with chores. Chores are often a source of parent-preteen conflict, especially when a job is unpopular, such as collecting trash. However, emptying wastebaskets is an appropriate job for a tweenager.

If your preadolescent is going to be the sanitation engineer at your house, sit down and the discuss the job. Estimate the amount of time the job will take on a regular basis. Discuss expectations; you and your child might view the job differently, so clarify acceptable standards. Then set a deadline for completion. In addition, offer your child the opportunity to accept this job for a certain time period. Your preteen might be garbage collector for a month, then be given the option to choose a different job for the next month. Also, encourage him to identify additional jobs around the house and suggest appropriate payment for the extra work. Sharing decision-making about chores can prevent a preteen feeling that he's overworked and underpaid.

Sharing decision-making about chores can prevent a preteen feeling that he's overworked and underpaid.

Be consistent in enforcing rules. Your child needs to know what to expect. One parent of a fifteen year old and eight-year-old triplets admitted, "I wasn't real consistent with our first one. About the fifth time she bugged me about something, I just gave in. I don't do that anymore because I can't. When the whining starts, I've made it a practice to say, 'If the whining keeps up, it will be punished.' That has helped a lot."

As you set rules, make an extra effort to be reasonable. Avoid limits that are unnecessary or unrealistic. Mentally put yourself in your child's place. Then ask yourself, "How would I respond to this rule?" Looking at rules through your child's eyes can help prevent problems before they happen. Unfortunately, though, as you'll read in the next section, not even the best-designed rule structure can prevent all child management problems.

Working Through Problems

Expect some conflict; it's inevitable. By the time a child is eight or ten, he has probably developed a variety of preferred problem-solving techniques. As one sixth grade teacher described:

"They get into a physical fight; pushing or shoving is

usually the case. Smearing and name calling is usually done behind the person's back.

"Notes are popular. A nasty note can be given directly to the person in class, given to a classmate to deliver or left in the other student's desk. The reason they write so many notes is that they don't verbalize well on a one-to-one basis when there is a problem. They are uncertain how the other kid will react if they say something; with a note, they don't have to worry about feedback from the kid."

Unfortunately, preteens who write notes might have to be concerned about negative feedback (punishment) from the teacher. Note writing, like some other tweenage problem-solving techniques, might create problems instead of solutions. That's why it's so important to practice at home, model at home, and teach at home various ways to solve problems. Often, preadolescents get into trouble because they do not consider more than one possible solution. Because your child now has the ability to think through situations, you can help him consider several ways to solve a problem.

For example, Dan is missing his geography book. He immediately accuses Chris of stealing the book. There is a brief tussle in the hallway, but after approaching the problem his way, Dan still doesn't have his book.

So at home he discusses the situation with his father. "Dad," he begins, "I don't want you to get upset, but my geography book is missing."

"Where did you last see it?" his dad asks.

"It was in my desk in homeroom. I know it was there."

"Where else did you look for it?" Dan's dad persists.

"I looked on the floor. It wasn't there," Dan answers.

"Did you ask your teacher if he had seen it?"

"No. I could ask Mr. Culbertson," Dan offers. "He's my homeroom teacher."

"Whom else could you ask?"

"I guess Mr. Hamm, my social studies teacher," Dan answers.

"Anyone else?" His dad keeps the questions coming.

"Some of the kids, I guess. Jeremy is letting me use his book tomorrow. Maybe somebody else has seen my book."

"Where else could you look?"

Dan thinks a moment. "Mr. Grabau has a box where he puts lost stuff in the science room. And maybe I could look at lost and found."

"Don't worry about it now, but let's talk tomorrow after school."

"What if I can't find it?" Dan asks.

His dad offers a specific solution. "We'll buy you a new book right away, so you can keep up in class. Then we can talk about ways you can earn the money to pay for it. But you've got lots of people to ask and places to look first, so that book might turn up, yet."

In this situation, the seventh grader used a typical preteen solution: blame another child and then fight. The father modeled verbal problem solving as an alternative to the inappropriate physical confrontation the boy had unsuccessfully tried. The dad also suggested several other solutions.

MIRROR
TALK

The biggest problem I have with my child is _____
_____.

We usually solve this problem by _____
_____.

One way I successfully avoid a problem is _____
_____.

One problem situation I handled effectively was _____
_____.

As your child works through potential conflicts, encourage him to solve a problem at the lowest level: if something happens, stop and discuss the issue. Don't let it grow into something larger.

Also help your child use his advanced thinking and communication skills. He has the ability to negotiate and mentally work through issues. Here's how one parent helped a nine year old use these skills to defuse a potential problem:

"Justin was driving a go-cart too fast. Apparently, he didn't follow the directions my brother had given him, and he had to take the cart back. Justin was crushed.

"He told me, 'I made Ralph upset.' Justin and I talked about this. I encouraged him to go and talk to Ralph.

"Justin said, 'It's so hard to do that.' I encouraged him again. I said, 'I know it will make the situation better.'

"He thought for a while. It took forty-five minutes before Justin got up enough nerve to talk to his uncle, but I could tell immediately when he had done it."

Justin was encouraged to talk through the incident immediately. There wasn't time for him to blow up the issue, either in his imagination or in conversation, into something bigger than what actually happened. Justin's parent helped him avoid the potential of a bigger problem. Some situations, though, can't be prevented or settled as quickly as this one. Every preteen needs to learn that inappropriate behavior has consequences.

Consequences of Inappropriate Behavior

The goal of disciplinary action should emphasize that a child's behavior is unacceptable and should not be repeated. Spanking or any other type of physical discipline is inappropriate for a preadolescent. Instead, you might say, "Go to your room for fifteen minutes." Or you might redirect him to another activity or location.

Another technique that is often effective with a preteen is to remove or deny a privilege: your daughter might not be allowed to watch a favorite television program or go out with friends after cheerleading practice or talk on the phone.

For this technique to work effectively, you will need to remove something that is important to your child. Saying to your child, "Since you didn't get your homework done before supper, you can't shoot hoops tonight," will be most effective when it's a pleasant evening and your child can hear the sound of friends at play. It would be ineffective if the weather is cold and rainy.

MIRROR
TALK

Looking ahead, one problem I anticipate facing soon is _____
_____.

One way I can prevent this problem is _____
_____.

When I think of punishment, I think about _____
_____.

When my child thinks of punishment, he/she might think _____
_____.

If you determine that some form of punishment is necessary, use these guidelines to insure your action will be effective:

Act promptly. Administer the punishment as soon as possible after the incident. One parent said:

"We were ready to go out the door to a birthday party, and Tara did something that was inexcusable. She begged, 'I promise to be good. Just let me go to the party.'

"We were ready to go out the door to a birthday party, and Tara did something that was inexcusable. She begged, 'I promise to be good. Just let me go to the party.'"

"I literally phoned the mom and sent the present with another child. I told the mom, 'I'm sorry, she will not be there.'

"I'm sure that mom thought, 'Couldn't she punish her after the party?' but I stood firm. Tara had to know she couldn't do what she did."

Talk with your child before applying a punishment. Always talk first. Remember, at this age, a sense of fairness is very important. Your child will very likely feel that she deserves a chance to be heard. Listen to how she describes the incident from her point of view. Then discuss. After that, apply an appropriate punishment, if necessary.

Match the consequence to the crime. A first-time offense does not deserve the same type of action as a repeated incident. For example, if your child forgets to park her bike in the garage because she came inside to take a phone call, a reminder will probably be adequate and punishment won't be needed.

Discuss an issue privately. Your tweenager is very concerned with how she appears to others. If an incident happens in public, make a simple statement which will immediately alert her to the incorrect behavior and promise quietly, "We will talk about that later." Then follow through with a private discussion. Never knowingly embarrass your child in front of others.

Although punishment might be necessary, approach this whole area of discipline with a positive focus: try to catch your child being good. A child will thrive when you emphasize the positives. Create an environment of acceptance, warmth, and caring. When you do this, negative behavior will actually feel uncomfortable to your child. He will probably instinctively want to contribute to a happy atmosphere.

Catch your child being good. A child will thrive when you emphasize the positives.

Apply this positive approach to punishment, too; instead of focusing on a punishment, consider targeting the behavior that results in conflict.

For example, you might set up a system to reward your child if he succeeds in changing a problem behavior for five straight days. Choose a reward that will be meaningful for your child: eating at a favorite restaurant, inviting a friend to sleep over, or practicing base running with you at the local baseball diamond.

Another method of dealing with problem behavior is to write a contract with your child. This approach appeals to preadolescents because everything is clearly recorded and, therefore, it looks fair. A major benefit of a contract is that the child assumes responsibility for her own behavior. Identify a single behavior or habit; then agree on the specifics of how and when it will be eliminated. For example:

Problem: Josh consistently forgets to put his clothes in the hamper.

Discussion of the problem: Josh and his dad sit down at the kitchen table to talk. They agree that it is reasonable to expect everyone in the family to put dirty clothes into the bathroom hamper. They define dirty clothes as anything that is worn more than two hours or anything worn outdoors or to a sports practice for any length of time.

Affirmation for solving the problem: Josh and his dad agree that if Josh puts all his dirty clothes in the hamper by nine o'clock each night for the next week, without being reminded, he can go out for pizza with friends after the basketball game on Friday night.

They agree that if Josh does not have his dirty clothes in the hamper by nine o'clock every night for the next week, his dad will take him home immediately after the basketball game on Friday night and he cannot go out with his friends.

They also check the clock in Josh's bedroom to make sure it is set at the same time as the clock in the kitchen, which will be used to verify the nine o'clock deadline. Josh and his dad then write out the specifics of their agreement, sign it, date it, and then post it on the refrigerator.

Wrap-Up

Helping a child move toward self-discipline can be especially difficult during this time period. After eight or ten years of disciplining, you may find yourself in a pattern of giving in to inappropriate behavior. I can easily fall into an "automatic response mode" by reacting emotionally, in the heat of the moment, instead of choosing one of the excellent techniques discussed in this chapter. My reaction triggers a similarly charged response in one of our children. Perhaps the reverse happens in your family: your child might begin the vicious cycle of reacting with emotions instead of rational thoughts. Fear of not being accepted by peers, jealousy of other peers, anger that her body has changed so quickly (or not changed as quickly as others), or dealing with a wide variety of other feelings can lie beneath the surface of preteen disobedience. The challenge to stay on top of discipline concerns is ever present during these years.

When you believe that your child can become self-reliant, your child will attempt to live up to that expectation.

But as you've seen, many problem situations can be prevented; others can be worked through with patience and discussion. When you believe that your child can become self-reliant, your child will attempt to live up to that expectation. The inevitable problems will decrease in intensity and number.

A Final Word

I wasn't ready to parent a tweenager. I had the knowledge, but I wasn't emotionally prepared to deal with preteen issues. That's why I wrote this book: so that you could face these years with knowledge *and* confidence.

> "I wasn't ready to parent a tweenager. I had the knowledge, but I wasn't emotionally prepared to deal with preteen issues."

You and I are parenting at a unique time in history. This is the first generation in which preadolescents and their parents have been threatened by the high-stakes problems we face today. In addition, we are parenting our children to deal with a life we can only imagine.

One futurist foresees, "We're moving into a new world. Renaissance, reinvent, and reengineering will be new words in the vocabulary." He predicts the three R's—reading, writing, and arithmetic, which have been expanded to the four R's to include recycling—will soon include yet another subject: reorganization.[1] That's difficult for me to imagine: my children, earning a grade for a class on "reorganization"? Others who look to the future suggest similar radical notions. But no one can guarantee their predictions.

I can't make many guarantees, either. I can't tell you that because you read this book your child will earn a higher salary when he grows up. I can't promise that your child will have better health, get more education, or even be happier than your neighbor's child down the street.

But I can say with certainty that by parenting your child effectively as he moves from age eight to age twelve you will give her the best possible opportunities these years can offer. You will parent now, in the gap between childhood and adolescence, so that your child is equipped to deal not just with today but with tomorrow as well.

One parent of a ten-year-old girl and twelve-year-old boy shared an important point: "At the beginning of a movie I saw recently, there was a man profiled who saw the future. Because of his insights, he tried to push everyone toward that future. Christopher Columbus, Thomas Jefferson, and my father were people like that.

"I'm the reverse. I see so much value in what we are discarding. I want people to look backward and see why some of these things worked for so long and worked so well. I feel my family is a dinosaur."

"By this time, nothing really surprises me too much."

We must parent with an eye to the future but use the positives of the past. You begin these "forgotten" years with many strengths developed over the years. As one parent of a ten-year-old boy told me, "By this time, nothing really surprises me too much." Perhaps you feel the same way. You know your child; you know yourself. You know your strengths and weaknesses. You bring a track record in parenting. In addition, you have shown a willingness to learn and grow: after all, you have read this book.

You have seen how much actually happens to your child during these years. This time with your tweenager can't be forgotten. There's too much going on! Neither you nor I can put parenting into the autopilot mode and take a break for a few years. Our children need us.

We must parent today.

Appendix A

Additional Resources

If you are interested in more in-depth information about tweenagers, two organizations have extensive data banks and resources:

The Center for Early Adolescence
School of Medicine
University of North Carolina at Chapel Hill
Suite 211
Carr Mill Mall
Carrboro, NC 27510
Phone: 919-966-1148

This is not a direct service agency but an agency designed to assist professionals serving children ten to fifteen years of age.

Search Institute
122 West Franklin
Suite 525
Minneapolis, MN 55404
Phone: 612-870-9511 or 800-888-7828

Search Institute is a nonprofit, nonsectarian organization with a mission "to promote the well-being of children and adolescents through scientific research, evaluation, consulting and the development of practical resources."

Appendix B

Periodicals for Preteens

During preadolescence, paperbacks and magazines replace the hardcover books of the earlier childhood years. Magazines, in particular, fit perfectly into the lifestyle of an eight to twelve year old: your child can take a magazine to read in the waiting room at the orthodontist's office or while waiting for the rain to stop so soccer practice can start. A magazine subscription makes an excellent gift for a preteen and can be a subtle way to encourage reading. Contact the publisher for a sample issue or review current issues at your local school or public library before ordering a subscription. Many youth-targeted periodicals are advertisement free; most are in full color.

During this time period, your preadolescent might develop specific areas of interest: model railroading, baseball card collecting, miniatures, military history, etc. Your child might also become skilled in a specific area: playing the piano or the drums, playing goalie in soccer, perhaps swimming. Some adult magazines in these special interest areas are suitable for older youth.

In addition, alert your tweenagers to a "kids' page" or youth supplement in the local paper. Generally, these pages are targeted toward teens or preteens and include advertisements.

Please note that on the following pages, I have listed a suggested age range for each publication. My suggestion is not necessarily the same age group intended by the publisher.

American Girl
Pleasant Company
8400 Fairway Place
P.O. Box 986
Middleton, WI 53562-0986
1-800-845-0005

Bimonthly; girls age seven to fourteen. This publication features stories about Kirsten, Molly, Samantha, Felicity, and Addy, the popular Pleasant Company dolls, plus activities and contemporary tie-ins to the past.

Boy's Life
Boy Scouts of America
1325 W. Walnut Hill Lane
P.O. Box 15079
Irving, TX 75015-2079

Monthly; boys ages nine to eighteen. Published for Cub Scouts, Boy Scouts, and Explorers, this magazine has the highest paid circulation figures of any children's magazine.

Calliope
Cobblestone Publishing
7 School St.
Peterborough, NH 03458-1454
1-800-821-0115

Five times a year. This publication discusses world history in themed issues (for example: Medieval Tournament, Ancient Baths, Navigation, etc.). *Calliope* is one of four periodicals published by the same company. All four magazines are uniformly excellent, ad free, and intended for the same age group, children eight to fourteen years old. Other magazines by this company:

Odyssey features space, astronomy, and the stars. Ten issues a year.

Cobblestone has monthly themes focused on American history. Ten issues a year.

Faces is a child's view of cultural anthropology, a study of peoples of the world. Nine issues a year.

Clubhouse
Focus on the Family
Colorado Springs, CO 80995

Monthly; ages eight to twelve. Published by Focus on the Family ministry, this magazine includes puzzles, activities, and faith building stories. Also published by this company: *Brio* (for teen girls) and *Breakaway* (for teen boys). Although these publications are directed toward high school youth, a mature twelve year old might like them.

Cricket
P.O. Box 387
Mt. Morris, IL 61054

Monthly; ages nine and up. This children's literary magazine includes fiction, folklore, nonfiction, puzzles, jokes, and poetry. It usually includes work by award-winning authors and artists and is good for expanding a child's reading interests and exposure to various authors. Also published by this company: *Spider*, intended for ages six and up.

Dolphin Log
Cousteau Society Membership Center
870 Greenbrier Circle, Suite 402
Chesapeake, VA 23320

Bimonthly; ages seven through fifteen. This is a specialty magazine directed to children interested in marine biology and waterways. For a child who likes dolphins and such, this is a good choice.

Highlights for Children
P.O. Box 182348
Columbus, OH 43272-4708

Eleven issues; ages three to ten. This must be one of the most popular pediatrician's waiting room magazines. Every issue is full of puzzles, games, and stories. Some preadolescents will think of this as a magazine for younger children, but they might sneak a quick look when nobody's watching.

Kids Discover
Box 54205
Boulder, CO 80322-4205

Ten issues; ages six to twelve (but children older and younger than this will enjoy it, too). Each issue is devoted to a single topic and loaded with well-written information and color pages. For example, an issue on the Roman Empire included a time line of rulers, diagrams of architectural ruins, explanation of plumbing (at the time of Claudius), and a colorful take-apart illustration of soldiers' gear that any fifth or sixth grader would love. Other topics have been earthquakes, pyramids, bubbles, and trains. I especially recommend it for visual learners or if your child is hesitant to read.

Owl
255 Great Arrow Ave.
Buffalo, NY 14207-3082

Ten issues; ages eight to twelve. The goal of this magazine is to "interest children in their environment and the world around them."

Ranger Rick
National Wildlife Federation
8925 Leesburg Pike
Vienna, VA 22184

Monthly; ages five to nine. The publication focuses on plants and animals around the world. This science magazine is perceived by many youth as something for "little kids," but eight and nine year olds still enjoy the excellent photos and colorful features.

Sports Illustrated for Kids
P.O. Box 830609
Birmingham, AL 35283-0609

Monthly; ages eight to fourteen. This colorful, popular magazine is great for kids who might not read a book or a more typical children's magazine. Especially suggested for youth who need extra motivation to read.

3-2-1 Contact
P.O. Box 53038
Boulder, CO 80322-3038

Ten issues; ages eight to twelve. One of the popular products put together by the Children's Television Workshop, this publication is brightly illustrated, with lots of art and articles on science, technology, nature study, and current events.

World
National Geographic
P.O. Box 98006
Washington, DC 20090

Monthly; ages eight to thirteen. This full color magazine includes the expected great photographs, but children will also find articles of general interest.

Zillions
P.O. Box 54861
Boulder, CO 80322-4861

Bimonthly; ages eight to fourteen. Children evaluate products that they eat, wear, or use. It's a *Consumer Reports* for children. Helps children learn to be careful, critical consumers.

Zoobooks
P.O. Box 85271
San Diego, CA 92138

Ten issues; ages four to eight. Includes marvelous, full-color nature photographs and posters, although many tweenagers might feel they have outgrown this magazine.

Appendix C

Recreational Reading for Preteens

Series is the key word to encourage recreational reading for tweenagers. When your child discovers a particular series he likes, he will probably read all of the books in that series. Then he will look for additional books by the same author or a series with similar features. For quick reference, here are popular preteen series:

"Adventures of the Northwoods" written by Lois Walfrid Johnson (Bethany House).
Set in northern Wisconsin in the early 1900s, these books tell of the adventures of pioneer girl Kate O'Connell.

"American Girls Collection" (Pleasant Company).
A historical fiction series with titles that focus on each of the American Girl characters.

"Best Friends" written by Hilda Stahl (Crossway Books).

A different "Best Friends" character is featured in each title.

"Choice Adventures" (Tyndale).

A "choose your own ending" format encourages kids to reread the various titles.

"Cooper Kids Adventure Series" written by Frank Peretti (Crossway Books).

Indiana Jones type adventure stories with archaeologist Dr. Jake Cooper and two young teens, Jay and Lila.

"Days of Laura Ingalls Wilder" written by T. L. Tedrow (Thomas Nelson).

Fictional accounts of Laura's life after the "Little House on the Prairie" series.

"McGee and Me!" written by Bill Myers and Ken C. Johnson (Tyndale).

These books retell the stories featured in the hit video series.

"Sugar Creek Gang" written by Paul Hutchens (Moody).

Bill Collins and his friends find excitement along the banks of Sugar Creek.

"Today's Heroes" (Zondervan).

Biographies of contemporary leaders including Colin Powell, Ben Carson, and Joni Eareckson.

"Trailblazer Books" written by Dave and Neta Jackson (Bethany House).

Adventure stories designed to introduce heroes of the past, including Martin Luther, John Wesley, Harriet Tubman, Amy Carmichael, and others.

"Twelve Candles Club" written by Elaine Schulte (Bethany House).

The everyday adventures of Becky Hamilton and her four friends.

Appendix D

Bibles for Preteens

Some preadolescents will choose a Bible based on features they want: an attractive cover, study helps, illustrations. Others will be influenced by peers or adult role models.

Many Bibles have been designed especially for preadolescents. For quick reference, here are some popular Bibles used by tweenagers.

Adventures in Odyssey Bible (Word)
For younger tweenagers, especially those who enjoy the Odyssey video series.

Holy Bible; Designed Especially for Children of Color (Children of Color Publishing Co. You may need to contact the publisher directly: 1-800-952-6657).
King James Version, with six portraits of African-Americans from the Bible and thirty-two illustrations.

Illustrated Family Time Bible (Thomas Nelson)
Designed for family reading and interaction, with Bible

quizzes, examples of everyday situations, and "What should I do?" questions.

Kid's Application Bible (Tyndale)
Designed specifically for seven to twelve year olds.

The King and the Beast (Thomas Nelson)
A paperback New Testament using the Contemporary English Version. Many special sections. Best for teens or mature preteens.

The New Adventure Bible (Zondervan)
Available in a variety of cover styles, translations, and colors, this includes numerous special features and study aids for kids.

The Picture Bible (DC Cook)
Known as the "comic book Bible," this Bible has colorful illustrations and simple text throughout.

Precious Moments Bible (Thomas Nelson)
Pastel covers with art by Sam Butcher.

The Teen's Topical Bible (Honor)
Quotes from the Living Bible organized by topics. Paperback.

The Wonder Bible (Questar)
Easy-to-read Bible without verse numbers. Includes introductions to sections and overviews.

Young Reader's Study Bible (Thomas Nelson)
Uses Living Bible text with numerous study aids and 1,000 highlighted memory verses.

Notes

Chapter 2
Physical Development

1. David Elkind, *The Hurried Child: Growing Up Too Fast, Too Soon*, rev. ed. (Reading, MA: Addison-Wesley, 1988), 31.
2. This statistic was presented in a pamphlet titled "How to Talk to Your Child About Sex," published by the National PTA, 700 North Rush Street, Chicago, IL 61611-2571.
3. The video this parent used was "How You Are Changing, Ages 8-11 from the "Learning About Sex" series. It is available from Concordia Publishing House, 3558 S. Jefferson, St. Louis, MO 63118-3968.

Chapter 4
Social Development

1. David Elkind, *A Sympathetic Understanding of the Child, Birth to Sixteen* (Boston: Allyn and Bacon, Inc., 1974), 69.

Chapter 6
Spiritual Development

1. Robert Coles, *The Spiritual Life of Children* (Boston: Houghton Mifflin, 1990), xvii.
2. *Children's Ministry*, November/December 1993, 18.

Chapter 7
School Life

1. Carolyn Wallace, quoted in Gerda Gallop, "Parent: Assign Yourself Role in Kid's Homework," *The Tennessean*, August 24, 1993, 3-D.
2. Maribeth Gettinger, "Children and Study Habits," part of a National Association of School Psychologists handout series, edited by Alex Thomas and Debby Waddell.

Chapter 8
Organization and Schedule

1. For more in-depth discussion of this cultural change, read David Elkind, *The Hurried Child*.

Chapter 9
Making the Break: Parent and Child

1. A widely respected baby-sitter training program is "Safe Sitter." Written and developed by Patricia Keener, M.D., "Safe Sitter" offers an excellent, intensive two-day experience and is available at hospitals throughout the country. Contact the Community Services or Education Office of your regional medical center or the Safe Sitter National Headquarters at 1500 North Ritter Ave., Indianapolis, IN 46219.

Chapter 10
A New Look at Old Issues

1. John Rockefeller III, "Money-Hungry Kids," *Jr. High Ministry*, November/December 1991, 21.

Chapter 11
Communication

1. For more information about honesty, refer to James Garbarino, et al, *What Children Can Tell Us: Eliciting, Interpreting, and Evaluating Information from Children* (San Francisco: Jossey-Bass Publishers, 1989). The discussion of lying begins on page 121.

A Final Word

1. Edward D. Barlow, Jr., President, Creating the Future, Inc., in keynote presentation, "Journey Toward the Next Millenium: Educating for the 21st Century." Educators' Conference '93, Asilomar Conference Center, Pacific Grove, CA, November 23, 1993, sponsored by the Lutheran Church—Missouri Synod California—Nevada-Hawaii District.